Dad's Joke Book

60 Years of Politically Incorrect Jokes

KEVIN N. TREVOR

© 2019 Wellingham Entertainment

Copyright © 2019 by Wellingham Entertainment, Inc.
DAD'S JOKE BOOK
60 years of Politically Incorrect Jokes
Author: Kevin N. Trevor
ISBN: 978-1-689441032

All rights reserved. Without limiting the rights under copyright reserved above, no part of this publication may be reproduced, stored in or introduced into a retrieval system, or transmitted, in any form, or by any means (electronic, mechanical, photocopying, recording, or otherwise) without the prior written permission of both the copyright owner and the above publisher of this book.

Table of Contents

Editor's Note 5
Preface 7
The Art of Joke Telling 9
How to Use This Book 13

CHAPTERS	JOKES BY THEME	KEY	PAGE
Chapter 1	ANIMALS	AN	15
Chapter 2	BAR	BA	30
Chapter 3	CLASSIC	CL	35
Chapter 4	CRIME	CR	54
Chapter 5	DOCTORS	DO	56
Chapter 6	GAY	GA	69
Chapter 7	GOLF & SPORTS	GO	78
Chapter 8	LAWYERS	LA	82
Chapter 9	MARRIAGE	MA	85
Chapter 10	MILITARY	MI	107
Chapter 11	PG RATED	PG	111
Chapter 12	POLITICS	PO	117
Chapter 13	RACE	RA	120
Chapter 14	RELIGION	RE	169
Chapter 15	RUDE & CRUDE	RU	183
Chapter 16	SEX	SE	204
Chapter 17	TOTALLY NUTS	TO	221
Chapter 18	WHORES	WH	225

INDEX 231
BACK COVER   Acknowledgements

Editor's Note

This collection of 1000 plus jokes just might be the greatest collection of racist, ethnic, homophobic, sacrilegious, vulgar and classic misogynistic jokes ever told in the mid-twentieth century. To some of you unwilling to look at the time frame during which they were told, they are utterly cringe-inducing if not downright vile, others may gain an awareness of the mores of the era. Younger readers like Millennials and Generation Z might find themselves scratching their heads and confusion at more than a few "overripe" cultural references possibly knowing they ought to be offended but not knowing why.

However we are confident we will be redeemed by the considerable breadth and range of hilarity. Included are some clean jokes with talking animals plus hundreds of good old dirty jokes to tell about Hookers, Rednecks, Priests and Arabs and perhaps most frighteningly, Marriage. Our 1000 plus joke collection has it all – a diverse array of jokes that will satisfy a wide range of audiences... notwithstanding the value of the book as a historical folk document.

Hopefully the ever-tightening knot of groupthink in our culture is loosening. So, as long as you're not reading this book aloud in the children's library section, your chances of messy encounters with the Thought Police or the "Vast Army of the Unhumorous" (to paraphrase Lenny Bruce) are relatively slim.

A wise man once said that there are two kinds of jokes, clean jokes and funny jokes. I hope you find these jokes funny.

Just look at the tough time irreverent and outspoken big-name comedians are having trying to connect with the brainwashed and disgruntled young college students. When you think about it, could a movie like BLAZING SADDLES have been made today? I wonder.

At present, the most politically correct segment of society is found with the snowflake types at colleges. I have read that famous comedians no longer perform at colleges as the students appear to be offended by PRACTICALLY EVERYTHING. If this book were to appear in a typical college campus most students would probably vanish into their safe rooms to recover their emotional stability.

In my opinion this book could be part of the beginning of a free speech movement, a movement that would help counter the extreme and intolerant positions held at colleges and elsewhere in this society.

If you like your humor unrestricted, authentic and raw, this book is for you.

This is a piece of history. Don't let it slip out of your hands.

Preface

My father was good at remembering and telling jokes, and perhaps I inherited a bit of his talent. I remember in the mid-fifties that when I heard a joke, it would frequently go in one ear and out the other. So I started writing down the premise and punch line of the jokes I heard in little pocket diary I kept primarily to remind me of appointments. I felt that forgetting a joke would be analogous to losing money.

With the jokes now firmly in my memory or in my little book, I found it fun to be able to recall and tell a doctor joke to some doctors, for example. I also found it helpful in contract negotiations in which I was involved. Negotiations are stressful, especially for the party who has little or no negotiating leverage.

I remember one instance where a particularly onerous clause was proposed by the other party. It was given a paragraph number—I forget what number exactly—let's say it was 14. I told a joke about a man who went to a whorehouse who was directed to Room 14. What followed was rather ribald and it brought down the house. Every time the other party proposed clause 14, it was met with laughter and derision by people on both sides of the negotiations.

With this book you will be able to tell selected jokes to selected groups such as your doctor, lawyer, and other professions and businesses, and to use jokes to relieve tension in business or social situations. Telling jokes can be genuine ice breakers. Buy the collection and use it yourself. Remember you can alter almost any joke or modify the characters to fit your audience.

Kevin N. Trevor

The Art of Joke Telling

Nobody gives you an instruction manual for raising children, running a marriage, performing in bed, or telling a joke. Well, maybe for performing in bed—but really, that's not the best way to learn. Practice makes perfect, as they say.

You can't be an ace in the bedroom from reading a guide alone, but maybe you can improve your joke-telling technique with the following pointers. These tips work for all jokes: clean, dirty, and get-ready-for-the-lawsuit.

Be Prepared

You can tell an off-the-cuff zinger if you're Henny Youngman. Otherwise, plan on a little planning for the best results.

Looking for a joke to spice up a speech or presentation? Do a little research in advance (you are holding a joke book right now, remember?).

Want to add a little verbal variety to your conversation? Add a handful of all-purpose jokes to your repertoire (or a combo—some all-purpose jokes and a few for selected listeners).

Either way, mastering the art of joke-telling begins with an understanding of joke anatomy.

Telling a Joke: The Setup

This is how you open. You can be explicit in signifying it's a joke: "Hey, have you heard the one about the three-legged cat?" Or you can take the stealth approach: "You'll never believe what happened to my neighbor's cat."

Jokes are short. You don't want your joke to turn into a two-hour epic saga—that's tragedy, not comedy.

That said, it's important not to rush. The most common mistake novice joke tellers make is hurrying through the setup—the part of the joke that leads up to the punchline. It's understandable: The setup is deliberately meant to create expectations. Your audience suspects they're being led down a path. They're a little uncomfortable. You're a little uncomfortable.

This is how it's supposed to be. Take your time. Paint a picture. Enjoy the tension. Even if the setup is a single line, let it unfold. Going too fast with your setup is like going too fast in bed: It's not satisfying. Slow down. This isn't a race.

Telling a Joke: The Punchline

This is obvious but very important: Remember the punchline. We've all been there. Someone's telling a joke. They do a great extended setup. You can't wait for the punchline.

Then, unbelievably, they flub it. They get the wording wrong. Or they forget and have to search their brains for the line. This is not funny.

Bottom line: If you want to tell a joke, run through it several times for practice in the car or in front of the bathroom mirror. Right before you tell it, say it word for word in your mind. You might feel a little silly doing this, but it's far less painful than screwing up your own joke.

Own It: Making a Joke Your Own

Joke telling is an oral tradition. That means you don't have to tell any joke as it's written. In fact, improvise away. Personalizing a tried-and-true joke is a great way to make it funnier.

Addressing a group of orthopedic surgeons? Try changing the identity in any insult joke to "orthopedic surgeon."

Do you think it's funny to impersonate a woman? All signs lead to yes, regardless of the joke at hand. But do check local ordinances.

Do you do voices? Accents? Make faces? **Go for it.**

On the other hand, don't be afraid to play it straight, if that's your strong suit. A joke delivered by someone who's earnest, dumbfounded, or deadpan can be twice as funny.

Make Them Laugh: Read Your Audience

Remember the time you told the hilarious Polish joke to the guy with the Polish wife?

You don't?

Maybe that's because the guy knocked you unconscious for insulting his wife. The **funniest** joke in the world isn't suitable for everyone. When we put this book together, we spent a great deal of time dividing the jokes into **categories**, in part to make it easier to find the right joke for the right audience.

Every time you tell a joke, take a moment to read your audience first. Is this a close friend? A new acquaintance? Business associates? Tread carefully. The same joke that makes your brother pee his pants might cause a co-worker to file a complaint with human resources.

Be a Joker

It's like everything else in life. You don't start out beating your buddies at poker, singing like Sinatra, or making them cry on the golf course. You learn.

The same is true for telling jokes. Ever watch someone who's always got a great joke up their sleeve, whether they're schmoozing with colleagues or delivering a eulogy? They're utterly at ease, right? That could be you, but it'll take practice (remember, just like performing in bed).

Many of the most brilliant stand-up comics often can be heard adapting classic jokes and formulas to current news, personalities and events. This maximizes impact and relevancy.

Will Rogers was doing this in the 1920's, back when John Wayne was just a surfer named Marion!

To be a great joke teller, you have to tell a lot of jokes. A lot of jokes. Some are going to bomb. And some are going to strike gold. Keep 'em coming. It isn't always easy trying to be the joker, but it can be a lot of laughs.

How to Use This Book

One of the primary purposes of publishing this joke was to give the reader the ability to find the right joke for the right occasion. To that end, the book contains two methods for finding the right joke for the right occasion.

The first method is to select a chapter. The jokes are arranged in thematic order, generally moving from mild to wild, as you browse through all 18 chapters. PG Jokes will be towards the front of the book, and really sexual and politically incorrect ones will tend to be found towards the middle and end.

The second is to use the index at the end of the book which lists many keywords found in jokes and on airport bathroom walls. The first two letters preceding the number in the index indicates in which chapter the joke appears. (Example **CL**25 or **WH**382) Go to the desired chapter, then flip forward through the numerically ascending list to access your numbered joke.

You could bring these **CLASSIC JOKES** up to date.

Many Jokes are classic ones that you will want to update or adjust certain names etc. depending on the particular group you wish to flatter or make fun off.

Please enjoy Dad's Jokebook whenever you need to lighten your mood or to find the right joke to lighten the mood of the group you're in.

CHAPTER I
ANIMALS

Parrots, Talking dogs and literate Monkeys are veteran comedy props that work well in mixed groups. Working in some "blue" material now.

~-~-~~-~-~~-~-~

A Texan finds the fastest camel in Egypt and offers to buy it. The Egyptian refuses because he wants to protect the blood line. The Texan persists and the Egyptian offers a compromise in which he will sell the camel to the Texas after he castrates it.

The Texan says, "Won't it hurt?"

The Egyptian says no and takes two rocks and hits them together and the camel's balls fall on the sand. The camel screams and runs off into the desert.

The Texan says, "I thought you said it wasn't going to hurt."

The Egyptian says, "It only hurts when your thumbs get caught between the rocks."   [6]

• • •

An engineer, doctor and lawyer are bragging about their dogs and decide to have a contest using bones to see which dog is better.

The engineer says, "OK, Slide Rule, do your stuff," and his dog builds a beautiful building with the bones.

The doctor says, "OK, Sawbones, do your stuff," and the dog reconstructs a perfect skeleton with the bones.

[AN]IMAL

The lawyer says, "OK, Shyster, do your stuff," and his dog buries the bones and fucks the other two dogs. [20]

• • •

There once was a Gaucho named Bruno

who said, "There is one thing I do know.

A sheep is fine, a woman is divine,

but a llama is numero uno." [34]

• • •

Did you hear about the queer spider? He couldn't keep his hands off his brother's fly. [35]

• • •

Know the difference between a tavern and an elephant fart? A tavern is a barroom and elephant fart is a baroooom. [41]

• • •

To view this "too hot to handle" joke—subscribe to our website www.DadsJokeBook.com. [51]

• • •

A man walks into a psychiatrist's office with a duck on his head. The duck says, "How do I get this nut off my ass?" [63]

• • •

Know how to make an elephant fly? Well you start with a zipper about this long. [Spread arms apart.] [66]

• • •

Know how to make a bull sweat? Put him in a tight Jersey. [68]

• • •

Know why an elephant has a 5 foot cock? He'd look ridiculous

AN IMAL

with 6 inches. [81]

• • •

What would you have with a moth ball in each hand? (Ball fists and spread hands) A big fucking moth. [84]

• • •

Husband and wife dress up in a cow costume to go to a costume party. The wife is in the back and the husband is in front. They are late as usual and so they cut across a field. Halfway across, the wife yells, "There's a bull running after us, what will we do?"

The husband says, "Well I don't know about you, but I'm just going to stand here and munch grass." [86]

• • •

A man wants to buy a hunting dog and is told that the best dog in the county is Blueboy. He sees the owner, who says he wants $25,000 for Blueboy. The man objects and they finally agree to go on a hunt to see if Blueboy is worth $25,000.

The men let Blueboy loose and soon he trees a 'possum. The man raises his gun, but the owner gets a stick and knocks the 'possum out of the tree and Blueboy screws the 'possum to death.

They put the 'possum in a bag and pretty soon Blueboy trees a wildcat. The man raises his gun, but the owner takes his stick knocks the wildcat out of the tree and Blueboy screws the wildcat to death.

They go deeper into the woods and Blueboy trees a bear. The owner can't get the bear out of the tree, so he climbs the tree and pokes the stick at the bear. Unfortunately, he slips and starts to fall out of the tree.

AN|IMAL

As he is falling he shouts at the hunter: "Shoot Blueboy - Shoot Blueboy." [92]

• • •

A donkey is put in a pen of pureblooded stallions on a temporary basis. Suddenly, the stallions smell a truckload of brood mares that are being brought over to be serviced. All the stallions start to paw the ground and whinny. So the donkey starts to paw the ground and whinny. One of the stallions sees him and says, "You don't expect to get any of this stuff, do you?"

The donkey says, "No, but I just want to make my presence known so I don't get screwed in the confusion." [93]

• • •

What do you give an elephant with diarrhea? Plenty of room. [106]

• • •

What did the elephant say when he was pulled out of the quicksand by the balls? "Thank you Mr. Ball and thank you Mrs. Ball." [107]

• • •

Know what an elephant with an afro looks like? (Reach for your fly and start to pull down your zipper.) [109]

• • •

A woman wakes up with an elephant in bed with her. She says, "My God I must have been tight last night."

The elephant said, "Well not the second time." [121]

• • •

A man wins a horse in a raffle and is shocked to find out how much it costs to board a horse. He finally negotiates a price with a stable owner of $10 per month and says, "Does that include shoveling out the manure?"

[AN]IMAL

The stable owner says, "At these prices, there won't be any manure." [128]

• • •

A man came into the doctor's office and complained about a sore elbow. The doctor gave him a brief exam and told him to return with a urine sample the next day. The man thought this was ridiculous so he got a urine sample from his dog, wife and daughter. The man returned to the doctor's office and gave him the sample.

A half hour later the doctor took the man into his office and said, "Your dog has rabies, your wife has the clap, your daughter is pregnant, and if you don't stop jacking off your elbow never will get any better." [142]

• • •

A jaded man went to a whorehouse and told the madam that he wanted something different. The madam thought a minute and said, "Try room 14."

The man went up to room 14, but there was nothing in it except for a brass bed with a chicken tied to it. The man waited a few minutes, but when nothing happened he called up the madam and complained. The madam said, "Try the chicken."

He did and when he came down he told the madam, "That was pretty good," and he would be back next week. A week later he came back and again said he wanted something different.

The madam said, "Go to room 15."

He opened the door but the room was dark. When his eyes got accustomed to the light, he saw that one whole wall was a two way mirror. On the other side of the mirror there was a daisy chain with three men, four women, and a donkey. After a few minutes, he whispered to the man next to him that this is really a weird show.

AN|IMAL

The guy next to him whispered back, "You should have been here last week, there was a guy fucking a chicken." [144]

• • •

In an early space program, a black was sent up in a capsule with a monkey. The monkey had a red phone and the black had a green phone. The monkey's red phone rang and the monkey made a course correction. The red phone rang again and the monkey increased the rocket's speed.

The black was getting mad, but finally his phone rang.

The message said, "Feed the monkey a banana." [181]

• • •

What do you get when you cross a bunny with a moose? The horniest bunny you ever saw. [182]

• • •

Know what you get when you cross a donkey with a peanut butter sandwich? Either a peanut butter sandwich with ears or a piece of ass that sticks to the roof of your mouth. [237]

• • •

A man was bragging about how smart his hunting dog was. His friend was skeptical so they agreed to go on a hunting trip with the dog. They get into the woods and the dog goes to the hunter and taps his master once on his knee.

The skeptic says, "What does that mean?"

The owner says, "That means there is one bird in the bush over there." They go over and, sure enough, flush one bird. They move on and the dog comes back and touches his master's knee twice.

The skeptic says, "What does that mean?"

ANIMAL

The owner says, "That means there are two birds in that bush," and, sure enough they flush two birds. This goes on and each time they flush the number of birds the dog indicated.

Finally the dog comes back and starts to hump his master's leg.

The skeptic says, "What does that mean?" The owner says, "That means there are so many fucking birds in that bush he can't even count them." [244]

• • •

Tom's cat is driving the neighbors crazy. He's out every night screwing and yowling. After the neighbors ask him to get rid of the cat, the owner offers to get the cat fixed. After a while, a neighbor tells him how nice it is with the cat not being out all night.

The owner says, "Oh he still goes out every night."

The neighbor says, "I thought he was fixed. What does he do?"

The owner says, "He acts as a consultant." [245]

• • •

Two fleas live in a beatnik's beard. They get drunk on the booze in the beard when the beatnik is kissing his girlfriend. They wake up the next morning and one flea says, "Do you remember what happened last night?"

The second flea says, "I don't even know how we got back home. The last thing I remember is falling down the front of that girl's dress." [253]

• • •

A man goes to the welfare office and tries to get his dog on welfare. The clerk says the dog doesn't qualify. The man says, "Why not? He's black, never worked a day in his life, and

AN|IMAL

doesn't know who his father is." [258]

• • •

A kid sees two dogs screwing and asks his father what they are doing. The father says, "They are making a puppy."

That afternoon the kid surprises his parents making love. He asks what they are doing. The father says, "We're making you a baby brother."

The kid starts to cry and says, "Turn Mommy over, Dad. I'd rather have a puppy." [262]

• • •

Boy sees a male dog on top of a female. He asks his father what the two dogs are doing. The father says, "Well, the dog on top hurt his paw and the dog underneath is his friend and he's trying to help carry him."

The kid says, "It happens every time. Try to help a friend and he'll fuck you every time." [289]

• • •

A man is sitting in a bar with a dog that has a sign around his neck reading, "I eat pussy." A woman on the next bar stool turns to the guy and says, "Does this dog really eat pussy?"

The guy says, "Sure," so they go to her room and she takes her clothes off and lies down on the bed. The guy says, "Rover, eat pussy." The dog just yawns.

This goes on four or five times so the man says, "OK, Rover, watch closely. I'm only going to do this once." [320]

• • •

A postman always seems to get bit by the same dog, so after the fifth complaint, the owner takes the dog to the vet to have him put to sleep.

AN IMAL

The vet says, "You don't have to put him to sleep, just neuter him and he won't be so vicious."

So when the owner gets the dog home he sees the mailman and yells, "You don't have to worry, I had my dog's balls cut off."

The postman says, "Why didn't you have his teeth pulled? I wasn't afraid he was going to try and fuck me." [321]

• • •

A man wanted to hire a private detective to spy on his wife but found they were too expensive. So he decided to buy a parrot. He went to a pet store and saw a parrot that was on sale for half price. He asked the owner what was wrong with him, and the owner says, "He doesn't have any feet so he holds on to his perch by wrapping his cock around it."

The man looked more closely and sure enough there was this little cock wrapped around the perch. He tells the parrot to keep an eye on his wife and to tell him everything that happens and then goes to work. When he got home that night he asked the parrot what happened.

The parrot said, "Well about an hour after you left for work this young man showed up."

The man said, "What happened?"

The parrot says, "He kissed your wife."

The husband then asks, "Then what happened?"

The parrot says, "He took off her bra and started to kiss her breasts."

The husband says, "Then what happened?"

ANIMAL

The parrot says, "I don't know I got a hard on and fell off my perch." [347]

• • •

An Indian, a Polack, and an Israeli came to a farm house asking for a place to sleep. The farmer says, "I only have room for two in the house; one of you will have to sleep in the barn."

The Indian says, "Cows are sacred to me. I can't sleep in the barn."

The Israeli says, "Pigs are forbidden flesh to me. I can't sleep in the barn."

The Polack says, "OK. I'll sleep in the barn."

About ten minutes later there's a knock at the door and when the farmer opens the door there are three cows and five pigs. [361]

• • •

An Israeli diplomat goes by a pet shop near the UN in NYC and as he goes by a parrot says, "Fuck Moisha Dyan." The Israeli goes into the store, buys the parrot, takes it home and cuts its tongue out.

The next day, the Israeli takes the parrot back to the shop and wants his money back as the parrot won't talk.

The day after that, the Israeli sees the parrot back in the window. The parrot sees him and gives him the finger and puts his other hand over his eye.) [386]

• • •

Drunk sees a woman with a duck under her arm and says, "Where did you get that pig?"

The woman says, "That's a duck, you stupid drunk."

The drunk says, "I was talking to the duck." [400]

IMAL

• • •

One black saw another throwing a dog up in the air and asked what he was trying to do. The first black says, "I paid good money for this bird dog, but I can't seem to get him to fly." [473]

• • •

Know what the elephant said to the naked man? "How do you breathe through that little thing?" [539]

• • •

Know what an elephant uses for a Tampon? A sheep. [572]

• • •

Know why an elephant has 4 feet? He'd look silly with six inches. [588]

• • •

What do you do with an elephant that has three balls on him? Walk him and pitch to the giraffe. [589]

• • •

How do you circumcise a whale? With four skin divers. [627]

• • •

Know what an elephant uses as a vibrator? An epileptic. [640]

• • •

A guest was sitting in the back yard of a friend and he saw a pig with only three legs. He asked his host what happened to the pig. The host said, "That pig saved my three-year-old from being bitten by a rattlesnake. It also woke me up when the house was on fire and saved my whole family from being burnt alive."

The guest said, "Yes, but how did you lose his back leg?"

[AN]IMAL

The host said, "Well you don't eat a pig like that all at once." [647]

• • •

A ventriloquist spent the night at a farmhouse and thought he would have some fun the next morning with the farmer.

So he goes out to the barn with the farmer and asks the cow what she thinks of the farmer. The cow says, "Fine except his hands are too cold in the morning when he milks me." The farmer is astounded.

He asks the horse what he thinks of the farmer and the horse said, "Well he doesn't really know how to saddle a horse." The farmer is amazed.

He asks a sheep what he thinks of the farmer. The farmer says, "Don't waste your time you know how sheep lie." [648]

• • •

A Czech and a Jew were walking in the woods by two bears and the Czech was eaten by one of the bears. The park rangers killed both bears and asked the Jew if the Czech had been eaten by the male or female bear. The Jew said, "The male."

The park rangers cut the male open but no Czech.

The moral is, never trust a Jew who says the Czech is in the mail. [747]

• • •

Frog looks out the stork's asshole and says, "How high are we?"

The stork says, "Ten thousand feet."

The frog says, "You wouldn't shit me would you?" [781]

• • •

ANIMAL

A devoted Christian is caught in the woods by some bears. He is much relieved when they cross themselves and pray, but then a bear says, "Dear Lord, for what we are about to receive, we give our thanks ... " [784]

• • •

Duck goes into a drug store and says, "I want to buy a condom."

The druggist says, "Do you want to put it on your bill?"

The duck says, "I'm not that kind of duck." [802]

• • •

What do you do if a pit bull humps your leg? Fake an orgasm. [837]

• • •

What's the difference between a pit bull and a woman with PMS? You can try to reason with a pit bull. [838]

• • •

What's the difference between a pit bull and a woman with PMS? Lipstick. [839]

• • •

A man sees a funeral procession where the hearse is followed by a man with a dog and 200 men are in line following him. The man asks, "What is going on?"

The director says, "This is a funeral for the mother-in-law of the man with the dog."

The man says, "How did she die?"

The director says, "The dog killed her."

The man says, "Can I borrow the dog?"

AN|IMAL

The director says, "Get in line." [873]

• • •

A hunter goes into the woods to hunt bear but the bear takes his gun away and fucks him in the ass. The hunter comes back with a bigger gun, but the bear takes the gun away and makes the hunter give him a blow job. The hunter comes back into the woods a third time with an even bigger gun.

The bear takes this gun away and says, "You didn't come here to hunt, did you?" [878]

• • •

Man comes into a bar and sees three guys and a dog playing poker. The man orders a drink and asks the bartender if the dog really knows how to play poker. The bartender says, "Yes he knows how to play, but he's not good at it."

The man says, "You mean he can't read the cards well enough?"

The bartender says: "No he can read the cards, but every time he gets a good hand he wags his tail." [891]

• • •

A baby polar bear asks his mother if he is a 100% polar bear. His mother says, "Of course. All your relatives on my side of the family were polar bears and your father is a polar bear."

The baby polar bear says to his father, "Am I a 100% polar bear?" His father says, "Yes all your relatives on my side of the family were polar bears and your mother is a polar bear."

The father polar bear says, "But why do you ask?"

The baby polar bear says: "Because I'm freezing my fucking ass off." [928]

• • •

AN|IMAL

Two guys were told by their wives to take the dog for a walk. The guys met on the street and decided they would rather go to a bar and drink. They went into the first bar they came to, but the bartender said, "No dogs are allowed in the bar."

One guy thought fast and said, "But this is my seeing-eye dog."

The bartender said, "OK, you've got a German Shepherd, but this Chihuahua can't come in."

The second guy closes his eyes and holds his arms out and says, "You mean they sold me a Chihuahua?" [936]

• • •

Know why Scotsmen wear kilts? A sheep can hear a zipper from fifty yards away. [1040]

CHAPTER 2
BARS

Are there things that don't happen in bars? Explore the mythos and drunken social aspects of bars.

~-~-~-~-~-~-~-~~-~-~

A bar owner is trying to hire a bartender. An applicant comes in and the owner asks for 3 references. He calls the first reference up. He says, "He's great bartender, but he'll steal you blind."

The owner calls up the second reference who says, "He's a great bartender, but he's drunk all the time."

He calls up the third who says, "He's a great bartender, but he's as queer as a 3 dollar bill."

The owner turns to the applicant and says, "If you steal so much as a penny, you're fired. If you take even one drink on the job you're fired, now kiss me and get to work." [25]

• • •

Drunk says to the bartender, "I would give $500 to kiss that blonde's tits."

The bartender says, "That's my wife." His wife hears about the offer and they both agree to do it, as they need the money. The bartender puts his wife and the drunk in a back room and the blonde takes her bra off.

The drunk starts to play with her tits and after 5 minutes the bartender says, "Well why don't you kiss them?"

The drunk says, "I would if I had the $500." [315]

• • •

A woman goes to a tattoo parlor and has Burt Reynolds' face tattooed on the inside of one thigh and Robert Redford's face tattooed on the inside of her other thigh. When the tattoo artist is finished she complains to the tattoo artist that they are not good likenesses.

Finally they agree that if a well-known painter who frequents the bar next door can identify the faces, the woman will be satisfied.

The artist takes a close look and says, "Well I don't know who the two guys on the thighs are, but the guy in the middle looks like Willie Nelson." [517]

• • •

Two guys are talking at a bar and they get interrupted by a drunk. One of the guys says, "Do you know I'm the architect who designed this building and if you jump out that window the design is such that the force of the wind will land you gently on that terrace 40 stories below?"

The drunk says, "You're full of shit."

So the guy jumps out of the window and lands gently on the terrace and waves to the drunk. The guy comes back up to the bar and says, "Why don't you try it?"

The drunk says OK, and jumps out the window and splatters himself on the terrace.

The other guy turns to the first guy and says, "You know Superman, you are a mean drunk." [554]

• • •

A guy comes into a bar and has 6 martinis and pulls out 2 twenties. He tells the bartender, "Here's your tip and buy a drink for that old douche bag at the end of the bar."

After he leaves the bartender says, "That man who just left was very rude but he did leave enough money to buy you a drink. Would you like anything?"

The woman thinks a minute and says, "How about a vinegar and water?" [567]

• • •

A gay is at a bar and he sees a handsome truck driver. He goes up to the truck driver and says, "Guess what's in this jar and I'll give you a blow job."

The truck driver is pissed off by the queer and says, "An elephant."

The gay slowly opens his hand and says, "I think we have a winner here." [580]

• • •

A rough bar in Houston has a gorilla bouncer. A big Texan came in and was thrown out by the gorilla. They had a big fight in the parking lot and the Texan beat the shit out of the gorilla. The Texan came back in, ordered a drink and said, "That's the trouble, if you give a n****r a fur coat, he thinks he's King Kong." [624]

• • •

A guy goes to a bar in Tokyo and says to the bartender, "I'd like a Stoli."

The bartender says, "Once upon a time ... " [828]

• • •

A gay goes into this redneck bar and sees this redneck with an alligator. The redneck hits the alligator over the head with a 2 x 4 and the alligator opens his mouth and gives him a blow job.

The gay tells the redneck, "That's the most amazing thing I've ever seen."

BAR

The redneck says, "Would you like to try it?"

The gay says, "Yes, but only if you promise not to hit me with that 2 x 4." [852]

• • •

To view this "too hot to handle" joke—subscribe to our website www.DadsJokeBook.com. [872]

• • •

Drunken woman, after six drinks, puts out her cigarette and says, "Tarbender, I want another double martuni and I think I'm having a heart attack."

The bartender says, "Look lady, I'm a bartender, not a tarbender. Second, those are martinis not martunis and finally you're not having a heart attack, your tit's in your ashtray." [893]

• • •

A man sees a good looking woman at the end of the bar. He tells the bartender to give the blonde at the end of the bar a double gin on the rocks and put in some Spanish fly. The bartender says, "I'm sorry sir we don't have any Spanish fly but we have some Jewish fly."

The man says, "OK, put some of that in her drink."

The woman accepts the drink and smiles and waves at the man every time she takes a drink. When she finishes the drink, she comes over and says, "Hi, good lookin' do you want to go shopping?" [949]

• • •

A man sees a pretty girl at a bar and says, "Hi good lookin' can I buy you a drink?"

The girl says, "Let's cut out all the preliminaries, I'll screw anybody, anywhere, anytime."

The guy says, "What a coincidence I'm a lawyer, too. What firm are you with?" [961]

• • •

A man goes into a bar and after a few drinks, asks the bartender if he would like to hear a Polish joke.

The bartender says, "I'm Polish and my two friends here are Polish professional boxers. Do you still want to tell the joke?"

The man thinks a minute and says "No. I don't what to have to explain it 3 times." [1043]

• • •

At a bar, a man asks the girl next to him if she would go out with a man like him. The girl says, "I might if he weren't too much like you." [1044]

• • •

A drunk at a bar says all lawyers are assholes. The man next to him objects and the drunk says, "Are you a lawyer?" The man says, "No, I'm an asshole". [1046]

• • •

What's the difference between a bartender and a proctologist? A proctologist has to look at only one asshole at a time. [1054]

• • •

A man and a woman exchange names, John and Mary, while chatting online and agree to meet at a bar. The man sees a pretty woman, who says, "Are you John?"

The man says, "Yes."

The woman says, "I'm not Mary." [1061]

CHAPTER 3
CLASSIC

While they may fade in direct sunlight, these jokes were written before any of us were born, and have evolved slowly into the memorable storytelling classics they are today. A little rework here and there and they are born again as contemporary classics.

~-~-~-~-~-~-~-~

Definition of a mistress: Something between a mister and a mattress. [1]

• • •

Definition of adultery: Two wrong people, doing the right thing. [2]

• • •

Gynecologist: Someone who spreads old wives' tails. [3]

• • •

Executive secretary: A girl who never misses a period. [4]

• • •

A gentleman is someone who wants to protect a lady from everyone but himself. [5]

• • •

Helen Keller doll: If you wind it up, it will walk into a wall. [7]

• • •

Mental health: Support Mental health or I'll kill you. [8]

• • •

CLASSIC

What has a 1000 legs and a cherry? 500 cocktail waitresses and a Manhattan. [9]

• • •

Hear about the new falsies made of M&Ms? They melt in your mouth and not in your hands. [13]

• • •

Did you hear about the flea on the toilet seat that kept getting pissed off? [16]

• • •

An astronaut lands on a distant planet and is shown around by a beautiful girl. She finally shows him the local hospital and says that babies on her planet are born in about a week. She asks the astronaut, "How are babies born on Earth?"

The astronaut proceeds to show her and to tell her that the baby will be born in about 9 months.

The girl says, "If it's going to take 9 months, why were you in such a hurry at the end?" [21]

• • •

Limerick: There once was a girl from Milpitas, who enjoyed intercollegiate coitus. She gave her tail to a halfback from Yale, but unfortunately got athlete's fetus. [28]

• • •

I don't care if you are Chef Boyardee. Get your balls out of my spaghetti. [30]

• • •

Did you hear about the traveling salesman who was so tired when he got home that he failed his loyalty test? [39]

• • •

CLASSIC

Know why martinis are like women's breasts? Because one isn't enough and three are too many. [40]

• • •

To view this "too hot to handle" joke—subscribe to our website www.DadsJokeBook.com. [45]

• • •

If you want to become a great lover, you have to learn to breathe through your ears. [52]

• • •

Did you know that horse shit is good for chapped lips? It doesn't really cure your chapped lips, but it does stop you from licking them. [60]

• • •

A man drove onto the Golden Gate Bridge and got out of his car and started to jump off. An ugly old woman appeared and said, "Don't jump, I'm a witch and I can grant you three wishes."

She finally convinces the man that she is a witch, and he says, "Well, first my wife has left me."

The witch says, "Don't worry, she's back at home cooking your dinner."

The man says, "I embezzled $100,000 from my company."

The witch says, "Don't worry, the money is back in your company's safe."

The man says "Thanks I'll go back to work."

The witch says, "Wait a minute; I did something for you, now you have to do something for me."

CLASSIC

The man says, "What?"

The witch says, "You must make love to me for your wishes to come true."

The man looks at the witch who is old, ugly and has a horrible smell. The man puts the witch in the back seat of his car and after much effort finally screws her. He says, "Now get the hell out of my car, you smelly old bitch."

The witch gets out and says, "How old are you sonny?"

The man says, "41."

The witch says, "Aren't you a little old to believe in witches?" [61]

• • •

What would you have if you had a large green ball in each hand? The Jolly Green Giant just where you want him. [85]

• • •

How many tigers can you get in a VW? I don't know but I've found I can't even get a little pussy in one. [99]

• • •

What do you get when you cross a computer with a prostitute? A fucking know-it-all. [100]

• • •

Know how to brainwash your girlfriend? Step on her douche bag. [101]

• • •

As the egg said to the water, "If it gets hot before I get hard, remember I was just laid this morning." [105]

• • •

CLASSIC

Hear about the gay with a black eye? He would rather fight than switch? [111]

• • •

Hear about the new aphrodisiac tranquilizer? If you don't get a piece of ass, at least you get peace of mind. [124]

• • •

Know how to wash a topless bathing suit? (stick out tongue and flick it.) [125]

• • •

How do you define a ratchet? Just like mouse shit only a little bigger. [130]

• • •

Girl comes into a bar and says, "Give me a fucking martini."

The bartender says, "You can't talk that like that. Let's change places and I'll show you how to order a martini." They trade places and the bartender says to the girl, "I would like a martini please."

The girl says, "Fuck no. You wouldn't give me one." [134]

• • •

Hear about the witch who bit her boyfriend on the ear? He turned into a motel. [135]

• • •

Know the difference between a mouse and a man? None, they're both looking for a little pussy. [138]

• • •

Behind every beautiful woman is a beautiful behind. [140]

• • •

CLASSIC

Mickey Rooney came up to a beautiful 6' Las Vegas showgirl and looking up said, "What would you say to a little fuck?"

The show girl looked down and said, "Hello little fuck!" [141]

• • •

Definition of a sanitary belt: A double shot in a clean glass. [162]

• • •

Hear about the queer Jew? Loved girls more than money. [163]

• • •

Hear about the angel who spread her wings and got a harp? Then she spread her legs and got an organ. [167]

• • •

Hear about the young starlet who thought ASCAP was a Greek prophylactic? [185]

• • •

Knock, knock.
Who's there?
Fuck.
Fuck who?
No, it's fuck whom. [193]

• • •

Do you know why they send Texas girls to eastern finishing schools? To teach them to say "that's incredible" instead of "bullshit." [197]

• • •

Bum asks an actor for a handout. The actor says, "Never a borrower or a lender be, Shakespeare." The bum says, "Fuck you, David Mamet." [207]

CLASSIC

• • •

Know how to tell a man with a bad kidney problem? He has a rusty zipper and yellow tennis shoes. [226]

• • •

Hear about the lawyer who got a sodomy charge reduced to following too close? [229]

• • •

A big girl was asked how she liked pantyhose. She said, "They're great, but every time I fart I blow my shoes off." [236]

• • •

Know the most useless thing on a woman? A guy about your age. [242]

• • •

Definition of a consultant: Someone who knows a 100 ways to make love, but doesn't know a single girl. [247]

• • •

Hear about the guy who lost a testicle and the doctor used a cocktail onion as a replacement? Every time he saw a martini, he got a hard-on; every time he screwed his wife, she got heartburn; every time his girlfriend gave him a blow job, her eyes watered. [268]

• • •

Definition of incest: Something the whole family can enjoy. [269]

• • •

A boy and a girl baby are playing in a play pen. The girl baby starts to yell, "Rape!"

The boy baby says, "Roll over, You're lying on your pacifier." [270]

• • •

Two guys met in a maternity ward. The first says, "This really makes me mad. I'm on vacation."

The second says, "You're mad? I'm on my honeymoon." [278]

• • •

Hear about the cute young girl that got so excited when she drank a Fresca that she snowed in her pants? [279]

• • •

A reporter asks Senator Kennedy about his presidential plans. Kennedy says, "We'll cross that bridge when we come to it." [287]

• • •

An old squaw gives a cowboy one vertical finger and one horizontal finger. The cowboy says, "What does that mean?"

The squaw says, "That's one for you and one for your horse." [288]

• • •

Definition of an avalanche: A mountain getting its rocks off. [290]

• • •

Little boy says, "I've got a 20' foot swimming pool."

The little girl says, "I've got a 30' swimming pool."

The little boy says, "I've got a 3 three-speed bike."

The little girl says, "I've got a 10 speed bike."

The little boy is getting pissed so he pulls down his pants and says, "Have you got one of these?"

CLASSIC

The little girl pulls down her pants and says, "No but my mommy says that with one of these I can get all of those I want." [304]

• • •

Know the difference between an old prostitute and a young one? It's the same difference as Polygrip and Vaseline. [305]

• • •

Kid tells his father he just got involved in his first sex act. The father is startled, as the boy is only nine. He says, "Tell me what happened."

The kid says, "Tommy threw a fucking rock at me." [307]

• • •

A salesman is stuck in Salem, North Carolina, over the weekend. He asks the bell boy where he can find the best sex in Salem.

The bellboy says, "There is a tree on the town square that has a hole that feels just like a pussy."

Late that night the salesman tries it and it was terrific. When the stores open, he rents a chainsaw and is just about to cut the tree down when he is arrested by the sheriff. When the salesman asks why, the sheriff says, "Don't you know it's illegal to take the cunt tree out of Salem?" [318]

• • •

Hear about the new drink? It's called "A Pleasant Surprise." It's a tit full of Scotch. [324]

• • •

Know the difference between pussy and parsley? Nobody eats parsley. [332]

• • •

CLASSIC

Know why the French "7" has a line through it? When God was trying to sell the 10 commandments to the French they drew a line through number 7. [358]

• • •

Difference between a streaker and a strutter. About 5 inches. [388]

• • •

Know how to get rid of crabs? Find a cocksucker who likes seafood. [393]

• • •

After a merger, one employee was asked what his new job was. The man said, "VP of sex and music."

Asked what he did, the man said, "Well I was told by the new CEO that when we want your fucking advice we'll give you a whistle." [398]

• • •

A wino goes into a grocery store and asks to buy some dog food. The clerk says, "Do you have a dog?" The wino says no and the clerk says, "Well you can't have the dog food, as it is not fit for human consumption."

The next day the wino comes into the store and asks to buy some cat food. The clerk says, "Do you have a cat?" The wino says no and the clerk says, "Well you can't have the cat food, as it is not fit for human consumption."

The next day the wino comes into the store with a paper sack and asks the clerk to stick his hand in the sack. The clerk does and pulls his hand out and says, "This is shit!"

The wino says, "Yes and I'd like to buy a roll of toilet paper." [406]

CL|ASSIC

• • •

Three most common lies: I love you. The check is in the mail. I won't come in your mouth. [435]

• • •

If it floats, flies, or fucks, rent it, don't buy it. [443]

• • •

Know why pigeons fly upside down over Dayton, Ohio? Nothing worth crapping on. [444]

• • •

A census taker is interviewing a hillbilly. The hillbilly says he has 11 children, but the census taker can only count 10. The hillbilly says, "One fell into the outhouse."

The census taker says, "Did you try to get him out?"

The hillbilly says, "No, it's a lot easier to just make a new one than to try to clean up the old one." [480]

• • •

Know why women can't drink beer at the beach? They get sand in their Schlitz. [488]

• • •

Quick responses: A grocery man says to his boss, "Some idiot wants a half a head of lettuce." The boss says, "I wanted a half a head of lettuce." The grocery man said, "Yes, sir. I've given you the other half." A new hire is asked what he thinks about Canadians. He says, "They're either whores or hockey players." The boss says, "My wife is Canadian." The new hire says, "Yes and what position does she play?" [495]

• • •

One woman is at a party where she swears so much that the other guests threaten to leave if she swears one more time.

CLASSIC

They start talking and the woman says, "Do you know the price of gold is so Goddamn high that there is a shitload of boat people going to Alaska?" All the guests get up to leave. The woman says, "Wait a minute. The fucking boat doesn't leave until Monday." [521]

• • •

Hear about the two bald-headed men who got so drunk that they stapled their heads together and made an ass of themselves? [534]

• • •

Do you know the difference between a stick-up and a hold-up? About 40 years. [553]

• • •

What do you get when you cross a potato and a prick? A dictator. [591]

• • •

To view this "too hot to handle" joke—subscribe to our website www.DadsJokeBook.com. [619]

• • •

Where do cousins come from? Aunt holes. [628]

• • •

Know why riding a motorcycle is like screwing your neighbor's wife? Just when you get good at it you get killed. [653]

• • •

Know the last thing that goes through a bug's mind when he hits a windshield? His asshole. [666]

• • •

Know the two things that smell like a fish? Want a hint? One is a fish. [667]

CL ASSIC

• • •

Know what Dolly Parton and Barack Obama have in common? Between them, they are the four biggest boobs in Washington. [668]

• • •

Know what a Valley girl puts behind her ears when she goes out on a date? Her heels. [669]

• • •

Know the difference between a moose and Lawrence Welk? On a moose the horns are up front and the asshole is in the back. [672]

• • •

Why is a 2-inch prick like a cobra? No one wants to fuck with either of them. [674]

• • •

What do a virgin and a hemophiliac have in common? One prick and it's all over. [675]

• • •

Do you know the difference between making love and eating asparagus? No? Let's do lunch. [679]

• • •

How do you know when your girlfriend is too fat? When she sits on your face and you can't hear your stereo. [680]

• • •

What do you call a virgin on a water bed? A cherry float. [693]

• • •

Know what the fastest 4 legged animal in the world? A baboon passing Loma Linda. [697]

• • •

CLASSIC

What do you call someone with AIDS and herpes? An incurable romantic. [704]

• • •

Know what everyone wants to get rid of in a penis? Wrinkles. [705]

• • •

Saint Patrick's Day in Beverly Hills is the day the Beverly Hills Jews watch their servants march. [707]

• • •

What's the difference between medium and rare? About 6 inches. [708]

• • •

What do you get when you combine a rooster and a telephone pole? A 30 foot cock that wants to reach out and touch someone. [710]

• • •

Know who is the Somali poster girl? Karen Carpenter. [711]

• • •

Know what the Jews in Beverly Hills call the San Fernando Valley? The "old country." [712]

• • •

Hear about the ritzy country club where all the wives think fucking and cooking are two cities in China? [713]

• • •

Know the difference between dark and hard? It's not hard all night. [715]

• • •

CLASSIC

Hear about Captain Hook dying? He had a bad case of jock itch. [716]

• • •

Know what you get when you combine the Pillsbury doughboy and a Cabbage Patch doll? An ugly doll with a yeast infection. [717]

• • •

Know what PLO stands for? Push Leon Overboard. [725]

• • •

What's the weather forecast for Chernobyl? 400 degrees and heavily overcast. So what do you use their mailboxes for? Microwave ovens. [739]

• • •

A widow woman finds a hinge on a gate to her backyard is broken. She takes the broken hinge to the local hardware store to buy a new one. When she enters, she sees a beautiful sterling silver tea set on a counter and she asks the store owner about it. He says it belonged to his mother who died but his wife didn't want it so it was for sale for $750.00. He then looks for a replacement hinge and when he finds it he says. "Do you want a screw for the hinge?"

The woman says, "No, but I will for the tea set." [755]

• • •

Do you have a nude picture of your wife? No? Well I've got an extra I'll send you. [756]

• • •

What do you call someone who's had a hemorrhoidectomy? A perfect asshole. [760]

• • •

CLASSIC

Hear about the 10 year old who told his 6 year-old friend that he found a condom on the verandah? His 6 year old friend said, "What's a verandah?" [761]

• • •

Oprah Winfrey was arrested at LAX. Customs officials looked up her dress and found 10 pounds of crack. [773]

• • •

Why did the pervert cross the road? Because his cock is stuck in the chicken. [775]

• • •

What's meaner than a pit bull with AIDS? The guy who gave it to him. [777]

• • •

Hear about the guy who was moaning about losing a relative at a Nazi death camp? When asked about it he said, "Yes, it was my uncle; he fell off a guard tower." [806]

• • •

Hear about the new disease CRS? (Can't Remember Shit) [807]

• • •

Did you know that in Leisure World, condoms are known as software and bras come in 36-inch longs? [815]

• • •

What do women's breasts and toy trains have in common? Though they were both designed for children, men like to play with them. [834]

• • •

A WWII vet was at a party and was asked his name. He said, "How soon do you have to have it?" [851]

• • •

Did you hear the Army is recruiting women with PMS to form a regiment and go to Iraq? They retain water and are meaner than hell. [867]

• • •

See June Allyson in that Pampers commercial? I remember when she was just wet behind the ears. [871]

• • •

An IRA agent is trying to buy guns from Khadafi but has trouble in making himself understood.

Finally after the tenth try at asking for guns, he says, "Guns, man, "G" as in Jesus, "U" as in onions, "N" as in knickers and "S" as in cement." [894]

• • •

Hear about the new Woody Allen film? "Honey, I fucked the kids." [900]

• • •

Know what Madonna's right knee said to her left knee? Nothing. They've never met. [901]

• • •

Know why women have two sets of lips? So they can piss and moan at the same time. [904]

• • •

Know how to get three elderly ladies to all say "shit" at the same time? Have a fourth elderly lady say, "Bingo." [906]

• • •

Blonde lives with another girl who gets two dozen long-stem roses from her boss. She says to the blonde, "I hate to get roses from my boss. It means I'll have to spend the whole weekend on my back with my legs in the air."

CLASSIC

The blonde says, "You mean you don't have a vase?" [963]

• • •

A ventriloquist's performance contained several jokes about how dumb blondes were. Finally a blonde woman in the audience got up and loudly complained about this. The ventriloquist apologized profusely for this and asked her to forgive him.

The blonde says, "I'm not talking to you. I'm talking to that little fuck on your knee." [976]

• • •

Three girls at a bar. The bartender turns to the redhead and says "What do you want?"

The redhead says, "S&S."

The bartender gives her a scotch and soda. He asks the brunette what she wants.

The brunette says, "G&T." The bartender fixes her a gin and tonic.

He asks the blonde what she wants and she says, "A 15."

The bartender says, "What's a 15?"

The blonde says, "Seagrams and 7 Up." [1020]

• • •

An Indian graduated from college with an electrical engineering degree. His outhouse had no light so he installed one. He became the first Indian to wire a head for a reservation. [1026]

• • •

If you hold a blonde up in the air by the ankles, what do you get? A brunette with bad breath. [1031]

Know the three things men like beginning with M? Mother, money, and Mmmm, pussy. [1035]

• • •

The boss opens his fly and asks his new secretary if she sees a private standing at attention. His secretary says, "No, I see a disabled veteran sitting on two duffle bags." [1038]

CHAPTER 4
CRIME

Convicts say the darnedest things! Go on a multi-state joke spree here. Only the nicest vices are featured.

~ - ~ - ~ ~ - - ~ - ~ - ~

Know the difference between standing up and being held up? About 20 years. [79]

• • •

Hear about the woman raped by an elephant? She was pregnant for 2 and a half years. [82]

• • •

Just after Bobby Kennedy was shot, Rosey Grier leaned over and said, "Do you have any last words?"

Bobby says, "Yes, Mary Jo Kopechne fucks." [296]

• • •

While in a restaurant, a man stabbed his mother with a fork. When the cops came to arrest him he socked the cop. Know what he was charged with? Mother forking and cop socking. [483]

• • •

Did you hear about the new honor system at UCLA/Florida State?

"Yes, your Honor. No, your Honor." [920]

• • •

CR|IME

Did you hear that after his trial was over, O.J. asked Judge Ito if he could have his glove back? [938]

• • •

Know the difference between Kato Kaelin and O.J. Simpson? Kaelin only *thinks* he's a lady killer. [939]

• • •

Know the difference between Mark Fuhrman and a black woman? Mark Fuhrman can get O. J. off. [940]

• • •

Hear that O.J. is moving to Arkansas? He heard that all the DNA is the same down there. [941]

CHAPTER 5
DOCTORS

He's the man who gets to see you naked without any dinner to buy, and he rarely makes house calls. These doctor jokes travel well and are available over the counter for your pleasure.

~ - ~ - ~ - ~ - ~ - ~ - ~ - ~ - ~

To view this "too hot to handle" joke—subscribe to our website www.DadsJokeBook.com. [11]

• • •

A wife is complaining about pain during intercourse. The doctor asks her to describe what starts the pain. The wife says, "Well there is this thing about 18" long and behind it are these two round things. What are they?"

The doctor says, "Well, I don't know about your husband lady, but with me they would be the cheeks of my ass." [47]

• • •

Man goes to a doctor and says, "I've got a case of flying crabs."

The doctor says, "There's no such thing as flying crabs."

The man pulls his fly down and one flutters out. The doctor grabs it and puts it under a microscope. The doctor says, "This isn't a flying crab, it's a fruit fly. You must have a dead banana down there." [69]

• • •

Doctor reaches in his pocket to take out a pen, but pulls out a thermometer. The doctor looks up and says, "Some asshole has got my pen." [87]

DOCTORS

• • •

A doctor was treating a wounded hunter and before he started sewing him up, said, "This will probably be the most painful thing you ever felt."

The hunter said, "This wasn't my most painful experience."

The doctor said, "What was?"

The hunter said, "I was out hunting and while I was taking a crap, my balls got caught in a bear trap."

The doctor said, "That was the most painful thing that ever happened to you?"

The hunter said, "No."

The doctor said, "What was?"

The hunter said, "When the chain ran out." [88]

• • •

A woman went to several doctors because of two green spots on the inside of her thighs, but no one could get rid of them. Finally she went to an old gypsy doctor who said, "You go out with a gypsy don't you?"

The woman said, "Yes, how did you know?"

The doctor said, "Just tell him to take off his earrings before gets in bed with you." [89]

• • •

A man is just admitted to the hospital and has to take a piss. He can't find a john, but finds a can and starts to pee in it. The can unfortunately contains some chemicals which explode. A nurse runs into the room and sees the man's ear is blown off and says, "I'll help you find your ear."

DOCTORS

The man says, "Ear? Hell, look for my right hand, it's got my cock in it." [91]

• • •

Man goes to a doctor and says that during intercourse he can't get it in. The doctor says, "Have you tried Vaseline?"

The man says, "No. Will that make it hard?" [136]

• • •

A man goes to the doctor complaining that he can't get his girlfriend to have an orgasm. The doctor says, "Well, next time you're making love, just when she gets close to having an orgasm, shoot off this gun and it should push her over the edge."

The man returns a week later and the doctor says, "Well how did it go?"

The man said, "Well it worked all right, but she also shit in my face and almost bit my cock off." [152]

• • •

Two men are waiting to see the doctor. It turns out one is there because he has green balls and the other because he has red balls. The guy with the red balls goes in first and when he comes out says, "I'll see you on the golf course."

The second guy goes into the doctor's office and after the doctor examines him he says he has to go to the hospital for immediate surgery. The second guy protests and says, "What's the difference between my case and the guy who is off to play golf?"

The doctor says, "It's the difference between lipstick and gangrene." [173]

• • •

DO|CTORS

A priest is at a hospital giving spiritual comfort to the sick. When the priest finishes his little sermon, the man is gasping for air and writes the priest a note before expiring. The priest thinks how glad he was there during the man's last moments on earth. He then reads the note which says, "Father you're standing on my air hose." [175]

• • •

A 60-year-old Polish woman goes to a doctor's office and asks for a birth control pill. The doctor says, "You don't need birth control pills."

The woman says she wants it to help her sleep.

The doctor says, "How will that help?"

The woman says, "I'm going to put them in my daughter's coffee." [221]

• • •

Man has a heart attack. The doctor says, "You'll have to lose 50 pounds, give up smoking, and get 8 hours of sleep each might.

The man says, "How about sex?"

The doctor thinks a minute and says, "Well, OK, but only at home. I don't want you to get too excited." [252]

• • •

A Polack has an IQ of about 90, which makes him too intellectual for his friends. The Polack goes to a doctor who says, "Well I can lower your IQ but you should be warned the process is irreversible."

The Polack says, "That's OK, I'd like to have an IQ of about 75."

The doctor says OK and puts a device on his head and turns the machine on. The doctor then gets a call from his wife and

DO|CTORS

before he can turn the machine off the dial has gone down to 60.

The doctor is all apologies, but the Polack says, "Don't worry, begorragh, 'tis a foine thing you've done to me." [263]

• • •

Hear about the dental patient who reached up when the dentist leaned over him and grabbed the dentist's balls saying, "We're not going to hurt each other, are we?" [264]

• • •

A couple comes into the doctor's office and tells him they don't think that they are making love correctly. The doctor takes them into an examination room and they have sex. The doctor says, "I don't see anything wrong."

The couple leaves but come back 5 more times.

The doctor says, "I don't know why you keep coming back, I don't see anything wrong."

The man says well, "A motel would cost $75. You only charge $50 and Medicare pays half." [316]

• • •

Man tells doctor that when he starts to make love he sticks it halfway in and everything gets blurry. The man says, "Then when I stick it all the way in I can't see anything."

The doctor says, "Well let's have a look at your organ." (Stick your tongue out.) [327]

• • •

A woman was nervous at the birth of her first child. The doctor, trying to relax her, says, "Just assume the position in which the child was conceived."

DOCTORS

The woman got into a contorted position with her legs over her head. The doctor says, "What are you doing?"

The woman says, "I got pregnant in a VW." [335]

• • •

During a medical exam, the doctor asks the patient if he enjoys intercourse.

The man says, "Infrequently."

The doctor says, "Is that one word or two?" [339]

• • •

During a medical exam a pretty female doctor grabs one of the guy's balls and says, "Say 99."

The guy says 99.

The doctor grabs the other ball and says, "Say 99."

The guy says 99.

The doctor grabs the guy's cock and says, "Say 99."

The guy says, "1, 2, 3, 4, 5, 6 ... " [343]

• • •

Man goes to the doctor and says, "I feel good but look bad."

Doctor pulls out a medical book and says, "Feel bad, look good, no that's not it. Here it is — feels good, but looks bad. My diagnosis is you're a vagina." [345]

• • •

Woman wants a facelift. The doctor says, "You can't have another."

The woman says, "Why not?"

DO|CTORS

The doctor says, "See that dimple on your cheek? Well it's really not a dimple it's your belly button. One more facelift and you'll have a Van Dyke." [373]

• • •

A woman slides down a bannister and gets a sliver in her pussy. She goes to a doctor who says, "I would like to take it out but I first have to file an Environmental Impact Report."

The woman says, "This is crazy, why?"

The doctor says, "You always have to file an E. I. R. before you remove timber from a recreational area." [437]

• • •

A man goes to Heaven and waits in line to get in. Another man with a stethoscope around his neck cuts in at the head of the line and goes through the Pearly Gates. When the man gets to the head of the line he says, "Why did you let that guy with the stethoscope cut in line?"

Saint Peter says, "Oh that was God, sometimes he just like to pretend he's a doctor." [445]

• • •

A doctor and his patient were golfing buddies. The patient felt ill and went to the doctor's office. After the examination the doctor says, "I've got good news and bad news. " The patient says, "What's the bad news?" The doctor says, "The bad news is, you're going to die."

The patient says, "What could possibly be the good news?"

The doctor says, "I shot a 72 last weekend." [469]

• • •

Three retired generals are talking. The first says, "I get up at 7 but I can't take a pee."

DO|CTORS

The second general says, "I get up at 7 but I can't have a bowel movement."

The third general says, "I have a good pee and bowel movement at 7."

The others ask, "What's wrong then?"

The third general says, "I don't get up until 9." [481]

• • •

A young lawyer at a N.Y. firm dies and, when he gets to the Pearly Gates, he complains to St. Peter that he was too young to die. St. Peter says, "That is strange. According to your time sheets you're 80 years old." [516]

• • •

A man is arrested for selling an Eternal Youth medicine on a street corner. The Judge asks if he has had any prior arrests. The man says, "Yes in 1720, 1859 and 1964." [568]

• • •

Know what you get when you cross a doctor and a zipper? A medfly. [620]

• • •

Three girls were complaining that they were going to die. One said she had the big C, cancer, the second said she had the big H, heart. The third said she had the big G, gonorrhea.

The first said, "You don't die of gonorrhea."

The third said, "You do if you give it to Mean Joe Greene." [637]

• • •

A middle-aged man who never married went to a sperm bank to make a deposit. The doctor gave him a jar and said come back with a sample.

DO|CTORS

A month went by and the doctor said, "What happened?"

The man said, "Well I used my right hand, I used my left hand, I hit it on the floor, I ran hot water over it, I put it on the radiator, but I still can't get the top off of this jar." [642]

• • •

Hear about the doctor who finally gets his patient on the phone? The doctor says, "I've got good news and bad news." The patient says, "What's the good news? The doctor says "You've got 24 hours to live."

The patient says, "What's the bad news?"

The doctor says, "I've been trying to reach you all day." [726]

• • •

A woman sees a man she likes so she pumps up her breasts with her arm. After a few drinks the man says, "How about going up to my place?"

The woman says, "Do we have anything in common?"

The man pumps his leg up and down and says, "Well, as a start, we must go to the same doctor." [785]

• • •

A doctor tells a patient that he's dying of cancer. He later hears the man tell people he's dying of AIDS. The doctor says, "Why are you telling people you're dying of AIDS when you're dying of cancer?"

The guy says, "I don't want anyone to fuck my wife after I'm gone." [822]

• • •

A man tells his psychiatrist that every day he drives to work on Beverly Blvd. and sees this gorgeous hooker. He says that he thinks about her all day and it is starting to affect his work. He asks the psychiatrist, "Can I take anything for this?"

The psychiatrist says, "Yes, take Melrose." [861]

• • •

An Irishman visits his doctor in Dublin and says, "Doctor I just don't feel well."

The doctor gives him a complete physical. He tells the Irishman, "I am sorry but I can't find anything wrong with you. It must be the booze."

The patient says, "That's OK, Doc, I'll come back when you're sober." [892]

• • •

An old man goes to the doctor for an examination. After about 5 minutes the doctor says, "You've got cancer."

After another 5 minutes goes by, the doctor says, "You've got Alzheimer's."

The old man says, "Thank God it's not cancer." [926]

• • •

Cops get a domestic disturbance call. When they get to the home, they go inside and see a man with a 5 iron in his hand and a woman is lying on the floor with her head bloodied and beaten in. They get all the background information and then ask, "Did you hit your wife with that 5 iron?"

The man says, "Yes."

The cops ask, "How many times?"

The man answers, "5, 6, 7, times. Put down a 5." [951]

• • •

DOCTORS

A woman goes into a drug store and asks if Viagra really works. The druggist says, "Yes it does. I use it myself."

The woman says, "Can you get it over the counter?"

The druggist says, "Yes, if I take two." [956]

• • •

A man walks into a dentist's office and says, "I'm a moth."

The dentist says, "You need to go to the psychiatrist 3 doors down."

The man says, "I know, but I was attracted by your light." [970]

• • •

Girl asked her boyfriend over for Thanksgiving dinner and said, "When dinner was over, she wanted to lose her virginity to him."

Guy goes to the druggist and says, "I want a dozen condoms as I'm going to screw my girlfriend's brains out."
Guy goes to her house for Thanksgiving dinner. He volunteers to say grace and delivers a long very religious blessing.

The girl whispers, "I didn't know you were so religious."

The guy whispers, "I didn't know your father was a druggist." [974]

• • •

A man stands in line at a bank, and when he gets up to the teller he pulls out a gun and demands money. The teller gives it to him, and he turns around and says to the man behind me, "Did you see me rob the bank?"

DOCTORS

The man says yes and the robber shoots him.

He turns to a married couple who are next in line and says to the husband, "Did you see me rob the bank and kill this guy?"

The husband said, "No, but my wife did." [986]

• • •

Dentist picks up a girl at a bar and takes her back to his apartment. He gets her in bed and then goes and washes his hands. She says, "Why are you washing your hands?"

He says, "Because I am a dentist."

After they finish making love, she says, "I know that you are a good dentist too."

He says, "Why do you say I'm a good dentist?"

The girl says, "Because I didn't feel a thing." [990]

• • •

A doctor was shaving in the morning and he, looked out the window of his Malibu home, and saw his Porsche 911 in the carport. He felt pretty good about himself. A good angel sat on his shoulder and said, "You should be ashamed, having sex with your patients."

A bad angel sat on his other shoulder and said, "Lots of doctors have sex with their patients."

The good angel said, "But they weren't veterinarians." [1000]

• • •

A man is being given a tour of a hospital with the hospital head. He goes by one room and sees a man masturbating. In the next room he sees a nurse giving a man a blow job. The man asks the hospital head, "Why the difference?"

DOCTORS

The hospital head says, "Better health plan." [1029]

• • •

A rabbit escaped from a medical lab. He enjoyed all the food he wanted, got all the sex he wanted, but went back because he was really dying for a cigarette. [1030]

• • •

An Irish woman is told by her doctor to bring in a specimen the following day. She got home and asked her husband what a specimen is. He says, "I don't know. I'll ask Murphy. He works in a hospital." He comes home with two black eyes and a split lip.

The wife says, "My God, what happened?"

The husband says, "I asked what a specimen was and he says, 'Go piss in a bottle' so I say, 'Go shit in your hat' and that's how the fight started." [1032]

• • •

A man tells his wife that his doctor told him he did not have long to live. The wife decided to talk to the doctor herself. She asked how she could prolong his life. The doctor says, "Give him all the sex he wants, prepare his favorite foods but have him avoid housework or work in the garden". The wife says "what if I don't follow your advice?" The doctor says "He will die." The wife comes home and the husband says, "What did the doctor say?" The wife says, the doctor says, "You're going to die." [1036]

• • •

Man asks a doctor if Viagra has any side effects. The doctor says, "Well, it may bring back your wife's headaches." [1055]

CHAPTER 6
GAY

All this diversity just proves God has a helluva sense of humor. These jokes explore the ever-popular "French Mistake," its players, and partners. Consider this the bowtie-optional zone.

~-~-~-~-~-~-~-~-~-~

First gay says to the second gay, "What do you think of my recent circumcision?" Second gay says, "It's marvelous. It makes you look 10 years younger." [26]

• • •

Three gays are arguing about their favorite sport or form of exercise.

The first says, "I like wrestling with all that body contact."

The second says, "I like ballet because it's so beautiful."

The third says, "I like baseball because of the recognition I get." When asked for an explanation he says, "Well it's the ninth inning, a tie score and a ground ball is hit to me in left field. I pick up the ball and the runner is rounding first, but I don't throw it to the second baseman. The runner is rounding second, but I don't throw it to the third baseman. The runner is rounding third headed for home and I've got 60,000 people yelling 'Throw the ball you cocksucker.'" [27]

• • •

Gay is out of work. Just as he is leaving to look for work, he sees his roommate jacking off in a brown paper bag. He says, "What are you doing?" The roommate says, "Well the least I can do is pack you a hot lunch." [32]

• • •

Two couples suggest that they switch partners. An hour later one guy says, "I wonder how the girls are doing?" [65]

• • •

Two Catholic gays who gave up meat on Friday. One ate fish. The other picked up a sailor. [119]

• • •

Pierre complains to his friend, "I, Pierre build the world's longest bridge, but do they call me Pierre the bridge builder? I build the largest dam in France, but do they call me Pierre the dam builder? Yet, if I suck just one little cock … " [122]

• • •

Two gays are walking down the street. One sees a dog licking his cock and says, "Gee I wish I could do that."

The second says, "Well, why don't you give it a try; it looks like a friendly dog." [196]

• • •

Gay goes to a gay whorehouse. He meets a gay named Schwartz who was the best lover he ever met. After a trip out of town, he went back and was told Schwartz no longer worked there but that they had an excellent replacement. The gay says, "No, when you're out of Schwartz you're out of queers." [208]

• • •

Know what an organ grinder is? A queer with a broken tooth. [215]

• • •

A man comes into the bar and says, "Do you know there's a gay in your bar?" The bartender says, "We don't allow faggots in here. Who is it?"

GAY

The man says, "You'll have to kiss me before I'll tell." [251]

• • •

Gay is driving a car and after hitting a truck, he gets into a fight with the truck driver. The gay says, "I'm going to beat him up." To the amazement of his friends, he does and then says, "What do you think of that?" A friend says, "Once a Tom Boy, always a Tom Boy." [309]

• • •

Definition of a good buddy. Someone who goes to Tijuana and gets 2 blow jobs and comes back and gives you one. [429]

• • •

Do you know there's a queer in the neighborhood? Do you want to know who it is? (Start to whisper in his ear and then kiss him) [470]

• • •

A golfer sliced into the woods. He didn't come out and a second golfer went in to find him. He didn't come out so the other two golfers went into the woods to look for them. They saw the second golfer buggering the first golfer.

When asked what he was doing, the second golfer said, "The first golfer had a heart attack."

The other two golfers said, "But you give mouth to mouth resuscitation for a heart attack."

The second golfer said, "Yes, that's how this all started." [472]

• • •

Hear about the fight in a gay bar? They went outside and traded blows. [492]

• • •

Hear about the new cereal Queerios? Put cream on them and they eat each other. [499]

• • •

Know what Rock Hudson got for Christmas? Steve McQueen. [540]

• • •

A gay went into a San Francisco deli and ordered a tongue sandwich. The owner said, "How do you want it to go?" [The gay sticks out his tongue and wiggles it.] [560]

• • •

Do you know the Oakland Bay Bridge is the longest bridge in the world? It goes from Africa to fairyland. [566]

• • •

How do you know a real bull dyke? When there is a kick starter on her vibrator. [570]

• • •

Hear about the Billy Jean dildo? It comes with a tennis racket handle and a watch that holds hands. [576]

• • •

Hear about the two gays each named Bob? They're known as the Oral Roberts. [578]

• • •

Hear Billie Jean retired? Yeah. She licked all her opposition. [584]

• • •

Hear about the Renee Richard's sex-change operation? It was a success until the anchovy fell out. [587]

• • •

Why do gays wear mustaches? To hide their stretch marks. [601]

• • •

Hear about the queer who got off for Jerry's Brown's lunch? [618]

• • •

Definition of panic: When a blind bull dyke loses her girlfriend in a fish market. [644]

• • •

Know what GAY stands for? Got Aids Yet? [646]

• • •

Know what you call a queer who doesn't have AIDS? A lucky cocksucker. [654]

• • •

Know what is worse than having your doctor tell you you've got AIDS? Hearing it from your dentist. [662]

• • •

Hear about the gay ecumenical conference? They were debating whether Jesus was divine or merely fabulous. [676]

• • •

Know what a gay parade is? That's when you swallow the leader. [690]

• • •

Know why Rock Hudson's insurance policy was canceled? He got rear-ended too many times. [718]

• • •

To view this "too hot to handle" joke—subscribe to our website www.DadsJokeBook.com. [719]

• • •

Hear about Rock Hudson's last wish? He wanted to be cremated and his ashes put in a fruit jar. [720]

Hear Rock Hudson is getting better? Yes, he's up on all fours. [721]

• • •

Gay asks his doctor for a cure for AIDS. The doctor says, "Go to Tijuana, order a large salad, two glasses of water, and extra Jalapeño chilies."

The gay says, "Will this cure AIDS?"

The doctor says, "No but it will sure show you what your asshole is for." [724]

• • •

Hear about the new disease, "Hearing AIDS?" You get it from listening to assholes. [728]

• • •

The good news is that Rock Hudson's wallet has been found. The bad news is that your picture is in it. [729]

• • •

AIDS research going slow as they can't get rats to fuck each other in the ass. [732]

• • •

Funeral service for AIDS victim: Ashes to ashes, dust to dust. If he only liked pussy, he'd still be with us. [733]

• • •

Hank Aaron has the most home runs. Pete Rose has the most hits. Who has been hit in the face with the most balls? Rock Hudson. [740]

• • •

GAY

Did you know that the Statue of Liberty has AIDS? We're not sure whether she got it from Rock Hudson or the Staten Island ferry. [745]

• • •

Hear about the four fags sitting in a hot tub? A bubble of sperm came up and the Queen said, "OK who farted?" [759]

• • •

Two gays see a beautiful woman. One says to the other, "Did you ever think of switching?" The other says, "Yes, I wonder what it's like to be a lesbian." [788]

• • •

Hear about the two gays who attacked a woman? One held her down while the other did her hair. [789]

• • •

What's the hardest thing about being a professional windsurfing instructor? Telling your dad you're gay. [790]

• • •

A gay recruit is being interviewed for serving in the Infantry. The sergeant says, "Are you capable of killing a man?" The gay thinks a minute and says, "Yes, but it might take several days." [811]

• • •

A gay is buying his new lover some shorts. The salesman says, "What size?" The gay thinks a minute and says, "This size." (Put three fingers in mouth.) [812]

• • •

What's the difference between a gay and a refrigerator? A refrigerator doesn't fart when you pull the meat out. [819]

• • •

What did one condom say to the other when they went into the gay bar? "I'm going to get shit-faced." [832]

• • •

Know how to get AIDS? By I.V. drug use, having sex with a gay, or by Magic. [888]

• • •

Hear about the fancy gay restaurant? They have a bread waiter, a salad waiter, a vegetable waiter, and entree waiter. For dessert, the head waiter comes to your table. [902]

• • •

Know the most feared words in the U.S. Navy? "Lights out." [909]

• • •

Hear about the Jewish gay? He wants to go into his mother's business. [910]

• • •

Hear the latest line at a gay bar. Come up behind a guy sitting at the bar and say, "Can I push your stool in for you?" [912]

• • •

Hear about the gay margarine advertisement? Is this margarine or butter? It's margarine, but it feels like butter. [924]

• • •

The Queen refused to go to her son Charles, 's second wedding. She doesn't believe in same-sex marriages. [967]

• • •

A man is walking thru Golden Gate Park in S.F. and sees the other man with his arms around a tree and his ear pressed up against the trunk. He goes over and says, "What are you doing?"

The man says, "I'm listening to the tree talk."

The man says, "Trees don't talk," and the other guy says, "You put your arms around the tree and your ear against the trunk and listen."
The guy does and says "I don't hear anything."

The other man says, "Keep listening," and puts a pair of hand cuffs on the other guy's wrists. He takes the handcuffed man's watch, ring, wallet, and keys and all his clothes except his shoes and leaves him there.

About a half an hour later another man comes by and says, "What are you doing?" The man explains what happened and the new guy says, "You can't get your arms back from around the tree?"

The other guy says no.

The new guy opens the zipper on his pants, kisses him behind the ear and says, "This is not going to be your day."
[988]

• • •

If homosexuality was a religion is would be called "Guyantology." If homosexuality was a cult, it would be called the "Cult of the Rama Butay." If homosexuality was a fantasy adventure novel it would be called "The Fellowship of the Two Cheeks" [1009]

• • •

Hear about the gay midget? He came out of the cupboard. [1033]

CHAPTER 7
GOLF AND OTHER SPORTS

Golf and other sports themed jokes are holed up here. That's right, it's humor in a jock-u-lar vein.

~-~-~~-~-~-~~-~-~

Three gays are arguing about their favorite sport or form of exercise. The first says, "I like wrestling with all that body contact."

The second says, "I like ballet because it's so beautiful."

The third says, "I like baseball because of the recognition I get." When asked for an explanation he says, "Well it's the ninth inning, a tie score and a ground ball is hit to me in left field. I pick up the ball and the runner is rounding first, but I don't throw it to the second baseman. The runner is rounding second, but I don't throw it to the third baseman. The runner is rounding third headed for home and I've got 60,000 people yelling 'Throw the ball you cocksucker.'" [27}

• • •

A golf club member is complaining to the other members of his foursome that his wife has cut his sex life down to twice a week.

His buddy says, "You shouldn't complain, I know guys she has cut off entirely." [97]

• • •

A 60 year old man is playing match play with a beautiful 25 year old girl. They hit it off and on the 18th green, the man says, "If I sink this putt, I'll take you to dinner."

GOLF

After he sinks the putt, the girl, who has a curling downhill 40' putt says, "If I sink this putt I'll go to bed with you."

The man says, "I concede the putt. Would you like to have dinner first?" [220]

• • •

After a particularly bad day, a golfer said, "The only two good balls I hit all day were when I stepped on the rake in the sand trap." [227]

• • •

A man wakes up early in the morning and rolls over and grabs his wife and says, "Well dear, is it the golf course or intercourse?"

The wife says, "Take a sweater dear, it's cold in the morning." [338]

• • •

Moses pulls a 3 wood out of his bag and just barely gets over a lake 220 yards away.

Jesus pulls out a 9 iron and hits the ball in the lake. He does this three times.

A friend of Moses says, "Who does he think he is, Jesus Christ?"

Moses says, "No, he thinks he's Jack Nickalaus." [446]

• • •

A woman goes into the confessional and says, "I want to confess two sins: I play golf on Sunday and miss church and I'm a hooker."

The priest says, "What are you going to do about it?"

GOLF

The woman says, "Well I thought if I changed my grip just a little…" [471]

• • •

Hear about the golf pro who was teaching a woman by standing behind her and holding each of her arms in his hands? Somehow his zipper got caught in her dress. They marched back to the club house, but before they could get in, a big dog came up and threw a bucket of water on them. [555]

• • •

A professor at a local college was lecturing on the subject of female anatomy and in particular on the subject of the female orgasm. To make sure everyone was listening to him, he said to a young woman in the front row, "When you are enjoying an orgasm, do you know what your asshole is doing?"

The young woman thought a minute and said, "He's probably out playing golf." [623]

• • •

A wife makes her husband promise to go to her funeral even if it's on the day he plays golf. The husband finally says, "OK, I will, but it will spoil my whole day." [880]

• • •

Know what a golfer can yell on a golf course but not in a whorehouse? "Bite you cocksucker." [890]

• • •

A man calls his wife and says, "It is too beautiful a day to work. I'm going to be home around 3 PM." When he gets home, his wife greets him at the door wearing a very sexy skimpy negligee.

She says, "If you tie me up, you can do anything you want."

GOLF

So the man tied her up and still got in 18 holes before dark. [977]

• • •

Know what a Monica Lewinsky putt is? All lip, no hole. [1057]

CHAPTER 8
LAWYERS

Jokes of and for the much-beloved legal clan.

~-~-~-~-~-~-~-~

A lawyer finds out his wife has a lover. So he writes the man a very legalistic letter concluding with a demand that the man be in his office on Monday next at 9 AM.

The man writes back and says, "I'm sorry but I'll be out of town that day, however, whatever you and the other guys agree upon is OK with me." [172]

• • •

An attorney was having breakfast and the plumbing went out. His wife wouldn't let him go to work until it was fixed. A plumber finally arrives and the attorney asks for an itemized bill.

The plumber gives him a bill for $55, $5 for a part and $50 for labor.

The lawyer objects and says, "That works out to $200 per hour. I'm an attorney and I don't get $200 per hour."

The plumber said, "I didn't get $200 per hour either when I was an attorney." [308]

• • •

God calls the Devil and says, "How about fixing the fence between Heaven and Hell?"

The Devil says, "You fix it you've got all the engineers."

LAWYERS

God says, "If you don't fix it, I'll sue."

The Devil says, "Where are you going to get a lawyer?" [424]

• • •

A woman asks her doctor whether you can get pregnant from anal intercourse. The doctor said, "Sure. Where do you think lawyers come from?" [787]

• • •

To view this "too hot to handle" joke—subscribe to our website www.DadsJokeBook.com. [792]

• • •

Two attorneys are walking down the street and they see a very pretty girl walking toward them. One attorney says, "Let's see if we can fuck her."

The second attorney says, "Out of what?" [848]

• • •

Did you hear the Iraqis have taken 500 American lawyers as hostages and are threatening that they will release one a day until we stop the bombing? [853]

• • •

Know the difference between God and a lawyer? God doesn't think he's a lawyer. [876]

• • •

Know the difference between a prostitute and an attorney?

After you're dead, the prostitute stops fucking you. [907]

• • •

A United Way worker approaches a lawyer and asks for a donation. The lawyer says, "I got a father who has Alzheimer's and my mother has incurable cancer. I have an adult son who has Down's syndrome."

The worker says, "I'm sorry."

The lawyer says, "You should be. If I don't give any money to them, why do you think I would give any money to United Way?" [997]

CHAPTER 9
MARRIAGE

Bliss or Battle, the many faces of marriage are wrapped up with humor, sex, sex, and more sex.

~-~-~~-~-~-~~-~-~

Bridegroom says to his best man the morning after the wedding, "You know it's a funny thing, my wife faints after having an orgasm."

The best man says, "Yeah, how about that?" [10]

• • •

Two married math teachers come back from separate vacations. The husband tells the wife, "I met a beautiful young girl, and though I'm 60 and she is only 30, we plan to be married."

The wife says, "Well, I have met a handsome young man, and though I'm 60 and he is only 30, we plan to marry. But, remember from your math classes, 30 goes into 60 a lot more often than 60 goes into 30." [12]

• • •

Guido says, "Hey Luigi do you like-a the girl witha the fat hairy legs?" Luigi says no.

Guido says, "Hey Luigi, do you like-a the girl with a mustache and a big fat ass?" Luigi says, "No."

Guido says, "Hey Luigi, do you like-a the girl with the big droopy tits?" Luigi says, "No."

Guido says, "Then why you fucking my wife Maria?" [24]

MARRIAGE

• • •

Man says, "Do you ever cheat on your husband?" Girl says no.

The man says, "Would you please hold my drink while I do?" [29]

• • •

A Jewish man wants to make sure his fiancée is a virgin, so he takes his prick out and says, "Becky what is this?"

She says, "I don't know."

Satisfied, he proposes and they marry. On their wedding night, he takes his clothes off and pointing says, "That's a penis."

Becky says, "No, a penis is 14" long and black." [37]

• • •

A man goes into the doctor's office complaining about a purple prick which he gets after intercourse with his wife.

The doctor says, "Do you wear a condom?"

The man says no.

The doctor says, "Does your wife use a contraceptive?"

The man says, "She uses a diaphragm."

The doctor says, "Does she use a jelly"? The man says yes. The doctor says, "What kind?"

The man says, "Grape." [49]

• • •

A Vaseline salesman comes to the door and asks the housewife if she uses his company's product. Wife is somewhat

MARRIAGE

embarrassed, but finally admits to using Vaseline during intercourse.

The salesman says, "Do you use the product?" The wife says no.

The salesman says, "Then your husband uses it." The wife says no.

The salesman says, "I don't understand how you use it. , please explain."

The wife says, "We put it on the doorknobs to keep the kids out of our bedroom." [55]

• • •

A man sees his doctor and says, "Doc, I think my wife is queer."

The doctor says, "What do you mean."

The man says, "She wants me to screw her in the ear."

The doctor says, "Explain what you mean."

He says, "Every time I try to stick my cock in her mouth she does this." (Turn head sideways.) [56]

• • •

The husband says, "How about making love tonight? It's our 25th anniversary."

The wife says, "No, I've got a big washing to do in the morning."

The husband says, "That's OK. I'll stop if I haven't come by then." [96]

• • •

MARRIAGE

The husband hits his wife's breast accidentally with his elbow and she yelps with pain. He says, "If your heart were as soft as your breast, you'd have a thousand lovers."

The wife says, "Yes, and if your prick was as hard as your elbow, you'd be one of them." [98]

• • •

Two 70 year old men each married 30-year-old women. The men met after their honeymoons. The first said, "I'm going to have to see my doctor, I just couldn't get it up."

The second said, "God I'm going to have to see my psychiatrist, I didn't even think of it." [183]

• • •

Man comes home tired and irritable. A customer cancelled a big order and he got into a fight with his boss. He finds his wife totally nude admiring herself in front of a full-length mirror. He says, "What the hell do you think you are doing?"

She says, "I went to the doctor today and he said that I have the breasts of a 20 year old."

The husband looks down and says, "What did he say about that 40 year old ass?"

The wife says sweetly, "Your name was never mentioned." [206]

• • •

A married couple's sex life was deteriorating. The wife went to a doctor and he said, "Take this pill every night before going to bed."

The first night the wife took a pill and the husband figured what the hell I'll take one too. In the middle of the night the wife woke up and said, "God, I need a man."

MA|RRIAGE

The husband woke up and said, "God, so do I." [212]

• • •

The phone rings and the husband picks it up. The voice says, "I'm the Boston strangler."

The husband turns to his wife and says, "It's for you." [217]

• • •

A man was undressing in a country club locker room and his friend noticed that he had a girdle on. He said, "How long have you been wearing one of those?"

The man said, "Ever since my wife found it in the glove compartment of my car." [224]

• • •

Husband was tossing peanuts in the air and catching them in his mouth. He turned his head and one got in his ear. Neither he nor his wife could get it out. His daughter and her boyfriend came by.

The boyfriend put his fingers over the husband's nose and said, "Blow." The peanut came out.

After they were gone, the wife says, "He's so smart, he ought to be a doctor."

The husband says, "From the smell on his fingers, he ought to be our son-in-law." [231]

• • •

An only child asks his parents if they ever have sexual relations. The parents reluctantly say, "Yes."

The kid says, "Well how come you never invite them to visit us?" [240]

• • •

MARRIAGE

A bar patron pays his bill and gets an entry blank. He asks the bartender what it's for. The bartender says, "You fill out the form and we have a drawing here at the bar. If you win, you get free drinks and get fucked all night."

The man turns to a guy on the next stool and says, "Did you ever win?"

The guy says, "No, but my wife has won twice." [254]

• • •

Husband says to wife, "Last night I dreamed I was at a pussy auction and some pussies sold for as high as $5,000."

The wife says, "Were any of the pussies like mine?"

The husband said, "Yes, but it wasn't for sale. " The wife asked why. The husband said, "They were using it to ice the beer." [276]

• • •

Husband says to his wife, "I can't understand it. The first time we make love I'm hot and sweaty and the second time I almost freeze."

The wife says, "That's simple. The first time is in July and the second time is in January." [293]

• • •

Onassis buys a basketball team with Wilt Chamberlain on it. He sees Wilt in the locker room after a shower and says, "How did your cock get so long?"

Wilt says, "I just hit it on the brass bed post ever night before I go to bed."

Onassis goes home that night and just before he gets in bed he hits his cock on the brass bed post.

MA RRIAGE

His wife looks up and says, "Where did you learn to fuck like Wilt Chamberlain?" [299]

• • •

A husband is screaming and moaning at his wife's funeral. His friend tries to comfort him and says, "I know it is hard to believe but someday you will find another woman to love."

The husband says, "I know, but what about tonight?" [301]

• • •

An actor comes home and his wife says, "Do you know that your agent was here and he ripped my clothes off, beat me, raped me, butt fucked me and then made me go down on him?"

The actor thinks a minute and says, "Did he leave any messages?" [302]

• • •

To view this "too hot to handle" joke—subscribe to our website www.DadsJokeBook.com. [312]

• • •

Husband brings his boss home unexpectedly and calls up to his wife and says, "I'm home dear. What are you doing?"

The wife says, "I'm upstairs washing my pussy."

The husband is embarrassed and says, "You shouldn't talk like that."

The wife says, "What do you want good grammar or good taste?" [313]

• • •

Wife comes home from the doctor's office and says that the doctor says we should have sex at least 30 times a month. The wife says, "Well, what are you going to do about it?"

MARRIAGE

The husband sighs and says, "Well, if it will help, put me down for two next week." [314]

• • •

Woman goes to the doctor's office for a physical. The doctor says, "I know this will shock you, but you're pregnant."

The woman says, "That isn't possible. I'm 60 and my husband is 70." She asks to use the phone and calls her husband and says, "Honey, the doctor says I'm pregnant."

There's a pause and the husband says, "Who is this calling?" [329]

• • •

To view this "too hot to handle" joke—subscribe to our website www.DadsJokeBook.com. [363]

• • •

A married couple agrees each can write the other's epitaphs.

He wrote: "Cold as usual."

She wrote: "Stiff at last." [374]

• • •

Husband tells his wife, "I'd sure like to get some strange stuff."

His wife says, "Well if your cock was more than 4" long you could get some strange stuff right here at home." [387]

• • •

Adam is walking through Eden with God for the first time. He says, "What's that?" God says, "It's a tree."

Adam says "What's that?" God says, "It's a flower."

Adam says, "What's that?" God says, "Deer."

MARRIAGE

Adam says, "What are they doing?" God says, "Making a baby."

Adam says, "That looks like fun. Where is my female?" God thereupon creates Eve and they go behind some bushes.

About 5 minutes later Adam comes out and says, "God, what's a headache?" [397]

• • •

A newly arrived war bride was unfamiliar with American customs during the Holiday Season. When the postman came to the house she takes her clothes off, has sex with him and then gives him a dollar and a full breakfast.

The postman says, "Lady, this was the most unusual experience in my 20 years at the Post Office. Could you give me an explanation." ?

The woman said, "Well when I asked my husband what to give the postman for Christmas, he said, 'Fuck him. Give him a dollar.' Breakfast was my idea." [402]

• • •

Young Italian graduates from High School in New Jersey. The son is looking forward to a watch, but his father gives him a gun. The son asks why.

The father says, "Son, you're going to college, you'll work hard. You'll get a job, you'll work hard. Your wife is going to get lonely and you're going to come home and find her in bed with another man. What are you going to do with a watch? Say 'Time's up'?" [426]

• • •

Italian couple had a big family wedding. Friends and relatives stuffed money in their pockets. One wealthy uncle gave them a $10,000 check and to make sure she didn't lose it, the bride put it in her glove.

MA|RRIAGE

After the wedding, the groom asked where the check was and the bride said, "I left it in my glove downstairs." As she didn't have any clothes on, she yelled downstairs, "Mom bring me my gloves."

The mother yelled back, "Be a good wife and take it in your bare hands." [427]

• • •

A mouse ran up a woman's vagina. The husband calls a doctor who says, "Put a plate of cheese next to your wife's pussy and maybe it will lure the mouse out."

He agrees to come right over and when he gets there he sees a plate of herring. The doctor says, "I thought I said to put a plate of cheese next to your wife's pussy."

The husband said, "Well first we have to get the cat out." [447]

• • •

A farmer was going through hard times. He is complaining to his wife that if her tits gave milk, he could get rid of the cow and if her pussy laid eggs he could get rid of the chickens.

The wife starts rubbing her husband's cock and says, "Well if this thing ever got hard we could get rid of The Hired Hand." [484]

• • •

George owed Jim a $100 so George stops by Jim's house and sees that Jim has got a very pretty wife. He tells her he'll give her $100 if he can screw her. She says OK and George gives her $100.

A little later Jim calls his wife and says, "Did George stop by the house?"

The wife is terrified, but says, "Yes why?"

MA|RRIAGE

Jim says, "Well George wanted to pay the $100 he owes me and I told him to drop it off at the house." [494]

• • •

Newly widowed Jewish woman has her husband's body cremated. She takes the ashes home and spreads them out on the coffee table. She then says, "Now I'm going to give you something you always wanted." (Blow the ashes) [512]

• • •

Know the definition of a Cad? A man who does not tell his wife he is sterile until she tells him she is pregnant. [532]

• • •

A Beverly Hills man called his home and the Mexican maid answers. He asks for his wife and the maid says that she is in bed and can't come to the phone.

The man says, "Wake her up."

The maid says, "She's not asleep. She's in bed with a man."

The man calling says, "You know where I keep the guns, get a gun and shoot them both or I will call Immigration."
A few minutes later the maid comes back and says, "I shot them."

The man says, "Where are the bodies?"

The maid says, "Well your wife is still in the bed, but the man staggered and fell into the swimming pool."

The man says, "I don't have a swimming pool, what number is this?" [564]

• • •

MARRIAGE

Farmer asked some newlyweds what they lived on. The bride said, "We are living on the fruits of our love."

The farmer said, "Well please stop. The peelings are choking the chickens." [635]

• • •

Know that many Jewish couples make love doggie style? The husband sits up and begs and the wife rolls over and plays dead. [682]

• • •

My wife is so frigid that when she opens her legs, a light goes on. [688]

• • •

A man tells his wife he is going on a hunting trip.

The wife says, "OK honey, I'll pack your clothes."

Two days later he comes back and says, "Honey, thanks for packing my clothes but I couldn't find any shorts."
The wife says, "I packed them in your gun case." [691]

• • •

Doctor tells a patient that he only has a year to live. The patient says, "What should I do?"

The doctor says marry a Jewish American Princess and move to Nome, Alaska. The patient asks why. The doctor says, "Because it will seem like the longest year of your life." [723]

• • •

Husband and wife confess. Husband says, "Every time I'm unfaithful I put $10 in this drawer." There's about $200 in the drawer."

MARRIAGE

The wife says, "Every time I've been unfaithful I put a golf ball in this drawer." There are three golf balls in her drawer.

The husband says, "We've been married 20 years and I forgive you."

The wife says, "Well, to tell the truth, every time I get 12 I sell them." [743]

• • •

Husband wins $10 million in the lottery. He tells his wife to pack her bags. The wife says, "Winter or summer?"

The husband says, "I don't care. I just want you out of here." [783]

• • •

Husband and wife stop for gas. Attendant says, "Where are you from?"

Husband says, "Kansas City."

His wife who is hard of hearing says, "What did he say?"

Husband says, "He wanted to know where we came from."

Attendant says, "I was in KC once. Had the worst piece of ass I've ever had."

Wife says, "What did he say?"

Husband says, "He thinks he knows you." [800]

• • •

Know the 3 words a woman doesn't want to hear when she's enjoying great sex? "Honey, I'm home." [810]

• • •

MA|RRIAGE

Husband comes home late for a party and finds his wife lying in bed nude. The husband says, "What the hell are you doing? We're late for the party."

The wife says, "I don't have any clothes."

The husband says, "You're crazy, you've got lots of clothes."

He goes to the closet and says, "Here's a red dress, a blue dress, Hi Harry, a green dress ... " [823]

• • •

On a transcontinental train an unmarried couple could only get on the train if they shared a compartment and the woman said, "Now it's important to act like we're husband and wife."

The man says, "OK."

The woman says, "Go get an extra blanket from the porter."

The man says, "Since we're married, get your own damn blanket." [826]

• • •

Hear about the man who was begging for a divorce? He finally said, "If you really loved me you never would have married me." [827]

• • •

Know the difference between a wife and a mistress? About 30 pounds. Know the difference between a wife and her lover? About 30 minutes. [830]

• • •

A Medicare-eligible wife tells her husband she wants a strawberry sundae, with whipped cream but without nuts. She says, "Write it down or you'll forget."

MARRIAGE

He says, "I don't need to write it down, I won't forget." A half an hour later he comes back with a hamburger.

His wife says, "You forgot the French fries." [836]

• • •

A man without a wife is like a statute without pigeons. [859]

• • •

Know the difference between a penis and a bonus? A wife will blow a bonus. [881]

• • •

A man is telling his friends about how when he went to get his social security benefits the clerk wouldn't believe he was 65. She finally demanded that he open up his shirt and when she saw the gray hair on his chest she agreed he was entitled to social security. When he got home he told his wife what happened. His wife said, "You should have opened your pants and you could have gotten disability benefits as well." [884]

• • •

The first night of the honeymoon the groom says to the bride, "Put on my Jockey shorts."

The bride says, "But they don't fit."

The groom says, "That's right and I want you to remember who wears the pants in this family."

The bride says, "OK. Put on my panties."

The groom says, "I can't get into them."

The bride says, "That's right, and you're not going to until you change your attitude." [914]

• • •

MARRIAGE

Hear about the husband who got in deep trouble with his wife? She asked him to go to the video store and rent the movie *Scent of a Woman.*" However he came home with "*A Fish Called Wanda.*" [935]

• • •

Wife wants a tit implant.

Husband says, "It's too expensive. Just take two pieces of toilet paper and rub them between your breasts for 2 months."

Two months later the wife said, "Dear, I don't think this is making my breasts any bigger."

The husband says, "That's strange, it's working great on your butt." [943]

• • •

The husband is on his death bed. The priest has just given him the last rites. He is restless and his wife is trying to calm him down. She says, "Just relax dear."

He says, "I can't." I have to confess something to you."

Wife says, "No you don't, just relax."

Husband says, "No I have to tell you that I had sex 10 times with your sister and 20 times with your niece."

The wife says, "I know dear, just lie there and let the poison do its work." [944]

• • •

Bum asks a business man for $5.00. The man says, "I suppose you want to buy booze with it." Bum says "No, I don't like liquor."

MA|RRIAGE

The man says, "Then you want to buy sex with it." The bum says, "No, I don't like women."

The man says, "Do you like golf?" The Bum says, "No, I hate golf."

The man says, "I think I'll take you home, have you meet my wife and give you a good home cooked dinner."

As they are driving to his home, the bum says, "I haven't had a bath in a month. I haven't had a haircut in two months and I haven't shaved in 3 months. Why do you want to take me to your home?"

The man says, "I just wanted my wife to see what someone looks like who doesn't like booze, pussy, or golf." [950]

• • •

A wife is entertaining her lover when her son comes home and goes into her bedroom. The wife puts her son in a closet. Then her husband comes home and she puts the lover in the closet.

The son says, "Christ, it's dark in here."

The lover says, "Knock that shit off kid. How much is it going to cost me to keep your mouth shut? The kid says, "Well I have a baseball for sale."

The lover says, "How much?"

The kid says, "$300."

The lover says OK and pays the kid $300. The next week the same thing happens. When the lover is put in the closet the kid says, "Christ, it's dark in here."

The lover says, "Knock that shit off kid. How much is in going to cost me this time?"

MARRIAGE

The kid says, "Well, I have a baseball bat for sale."

The lover says, "How much." The kid says, "$700."

The lover pays.

That weekend the husband says to the kid, "Let's play some baseball."

The kid says, "I can't, I sold my ball and bat."

The father says, "How much did you get for them?"

The kid says, "Well I got $300 for the ball and $700 for the bat."

The husband says, "That's gouging. I want you to go to confessional this Sunday and confess to the sin of greed." On Sunday the kid goes to church and into the confessional. He says, "Christ, its dark in here."

The priest says, "Knock that shit off, kid." [952]

• • •

Mexican opens first Mexican restaurant in Kansas. Two wives decide to go for ladies' night out. They have free margaritas and the ladies drink two pitchers full. They start to walk home and then both realize they have to pee. They are walking next to a graveyard and decide to pee behind the gravestones. They then realize they have no toilet paper. One wife uses her panties to dry herself and throws them away. The other wife has no panties and so grabs a ribbon from a new grave and uses it.

The next morning their husbands are talking and one says, "I don't think we should let our wives go to that new Mexican restaurant again. My wife came home with no panties."

MARRIAGE

The other husband says, "You think that's bad, my wife came home with a card in the cheeks of her ass that said 'From all the guys at fire station 5, we'll never forget you.'" [962]

• • •

Wife, who likes fast cars, told her husband that she wanted something that goes from 0 to 160 in less than 10 seconds. He bought her a bathroom scale. Funeral services are pending. [969]

• • •

Wife comes out of the shower and says, "I look old, wrinkled, and fat." She turns to husband and says, "Say something nice about me."

Husband says, "Your eyesight is damn near perfect."

Funeral services are pending. [973]

• • •

An older man has lost his wife in a shopping mall. He sees this beautiful young girl in a revealing blouse and short-shorts. He goes up to her and says, "Could you talk to me for a minute?"

The young woman says, "Certainly, but why?"

The older man says, "Well whenever I talk to a beautiful young girl like you, my wife suddenly appears as if by magic." [989]

• • •

A woman who has been married a long time feels guilty and says to her husband, "Dear, I'm having an affair."

The husband says, "Are you having it catered?" [991]

• • •

The Mexican maid comes up to the lady of the house and asks for more money.

MARRIAGE

The wife says, "Why should I pay you more money?"

The maid says, "Because I clean better than you do."

The wife says, "Who told you that?"

The maid says, "Your husband."

The wife says, "Anything else?"

The maid says, "Yes, I'm a better cook than you."

The wife says, "Who told you that?"

The maid says, "Your husband."

The wife says, "Anything else?"

The maid says, "Yes, I'm better in bed than you."

The wife says, "Did my husband tell you that?"

The maid says, "No, the gardener told me that."

The wife thinks a minute and says, "How much more a month do you want?" [1005]

• • •

Husband is arguing with the cop about a speeding ticket. The cop turns to the wife and says, "Can you do anything with him?"

The wife says, "I learned never to argue with him when he's been drinking." [1018]

• • •

Cop says, "Why were you speeding?"

MARRIAGE

Man says, "My wife ran off with a guy in the CHP and I thought he was trying to give her back." [1019]

• • •

Husband is in bed reading a book. When he is reading, he periodically runs a finger through his wife's vagina.

She gets aroused after a while and says, "What are you doing?"

The husband says, "I'm wetting my finger before I turn a page.".

The wife says, "Have you ever thought about speed reading?" [1024]

• • •

On her fiftieth anniversary, a wife puts on the same negligee as she wore on their honeymoon. She says, "Do you remember on our honeymoon you said you were going to suck my tits dry and fuck my brains out?" The husband says, "Yes."

The wife says, "What do you say now?"

The husband says, "Mission accomplished." [1025]

• • •

A man is on his death bed and he asks his wife if she ever cheated on him. The wife says, "Remember when we were first married and you got fired? Then after I talked to your boss you got rehired with a raise?" Then she says, "Remember when you started your own business and couldn't get a bank loan until I talked to your banker? And remember when you ran for the board of directors of Big Canyon Country Club and you were behind by 10 votes and won by 35? What do you think?" [1034]

• • •

MARRIAGE

Secret of a long happy marriage: Once a week have a long romantic dinner. I have mine on Wednesday and my wife goes out on Friday. [1039]

• • •

A 70 year old man marries a 30 year-old woman. The first time they make love, his cock starts to slowly drip. He rushes to the doctor's office and asks if he got the clap.

The doctor examines him and says "Do you remember where your wife lives?"

The man says, "Yes."

The doctor says, "Well you better hurry back there you're starting to come." [1050]

• • •

You know you are old when you don't care where your wife goes during the day as long as you don't have to go with her. [1052]

• • •

The husband loses his cock in an accident. He goes to a doctor who says he can replace his penis with a new 6-inch penis for $6000 or a new 10-inch penis for $10,000. The husband says, "I have to ask my wife which she wants."

He goes home and comes back to the doctor's office and the doctor says, "What did your wife say?"

The man says, "She would rather redo the kitchen." [1058]

CHAPTER 10
MILITARY

General humor, dispatched and appointed to this chapter, then declassified so you can enjoy every tally ho as it was spoken on the battlefield.

~-~-~-~-~-~-~-~-~-~

The British and American armies were holding joint military exercises. An American paratrooper jumped, but his parachute didn't open and a British paratrooper grabbed him as he came by. (Demonstrate with arms) The Brit looked down and said, "American?" The American said, "Yes."

The Brit said, "Homosexual?" The American said no.

The Brit said, "Pity." (Open arms.) [62]

• • •

A private keeps getting buggered by a corporal, but each time he complains, the charges are dismissed for lack of evidence. Finally, once in the shower, the corporal sticks it in his ass when he is bent over to pick up the soap. The private straightens up, pulls his cheeks together [walk with a tight ass] and says, "We're going to see the Captain." [110]

• • •

A customer relations man meets a general at the airport and takes him to his hotel room. He says, "General, here's the bar with your favorite whiskey." Pointing to a big buffet table he says, "Here's some great food, is there anything else I can get you?"

The general says, "I want a big-tittied blonde."

MI|LITARY

The rep gets on the phone and says, "Trixie, come to room 222 at the Airport Hilton." The customer relations man leaves.

About a half hour later, Trixie shows up and says, "What can I do for you, general?"

The general says, "Make me a whiskey on the rocks."

Trixie gives him the drink and says, "Anything else I can do?"

The general says, "Give me a blow job."

Trixie comes over picks up the general's cock and blows on it.

The general says, "No, Trixie, I want a blow job."

Trixie blows on his cock. The general calls the rep and tells him to get back to the Hilton.

The rep knocks and comes in. The general says, "Trixie, give me a blow job."

Trixie picks up the general's cock and blows on it.

The rep says, "Trixie, watch closely. I'm only going to do this once." [123]

• • •

During W.W.II a GI, after 6 weeks, asked an Arab what he did for sex. The Arab said, "Well you could rent my camel." The GI was horrified and said no.

Another 6 weeks went by and the GI got so horny that he went back to the Arab and after some haggling, he agreed to rent the camel for a weekend for $50. The GI backed the camel up to a stepladder and started screwing it. Some of his buddies saw him and started to laugh.

The GI said, "What are you laughing at? You rent this camel."

MI|LITARY

His buddies said, "Yeah, but we use it to get to the next town where the women are." [143]

• • •

A Scottish officer is inspecting his troops and as he passes one soldier he notices that he has a tremendous erection under his kilt. The officer turns to the sergeant major and says, "Give this man a 24 hour pass." A week later during the inspection he notices the same thing, so he tells the sergeant major, "Give this man a 48 hour pass." A week later he holds inspection and the soldier still has the big hard on sticking out from under his kilt. The officer tells the sergeant to find out what's wrong with this man and report to him after the regiment was dismissed.

The sergeant major reports to the officer's quarters and says, "Begging the colonel's pardon, but it's you he likes." [146]

• • •

Colonel got drunk at the Officer's Club and puked all over his uniform. Embarrassed he told his orderly that a drunken sergeant had vomited on his uniform and that he was going to give the sergeant 30 days in the brig.

The next day the orderly said, "Sir, you ought to give that sergeant 60 days."

The colonel says, "Why?"

The orderly says, "He also crapped in your pants." [274]

• • •

During the last days of the war Hitler asks his staff why they lost the war.

Goering says, "Not enough planes." Von Runstead says, "Not enough tanks."

MILITARY

Doenitz says, "Not enough submarines."

Hitler listens and finally says, "Well next time, no more Mr. Nice Guy." [506]

• • •

ACTUAL MILITARY FITNESS REPORTS:
• *He set modest goals and failed to meet them.*
• *As long as he is on my ship, some village will be deprived of its idiot.*
• *He used my ship to carry his genitals from port to port and my officers to carry him from bar to bar.* [1023]

CHAPTER II
PG RATED

Safe as houses, you can tell these PG-rated jokes to most moms, dads, bosses, any gathering of business people, and friends and relatives with a low chance of offense.

~ - ~ - ~ - ~ - - ~ - ~~ - ~ - ~

Two hobos get a housewife to feed them in exchange for cutting firewood. Suddenly one hobo jumps in the air, does pirouettes and back flips, and then does an impression of a dying swan. The housewife says to the other hobo that if the hobo on the ground would repeat his performance for her bridge club she would pay him $10.00.

The second hobo turns to his friend who is still on the ground and says, "Harry would you agree to get hit in the nuts with a piece of kindling again for $10.00?" [71]

• • •

A boy was born but his body was just his head. A genie gave him one wish. The boy said he wished he could dance, so the genie changed him into a foot. The moral is to quit when you're a head. [104]

• • •

Guy goes steady with two girls, Kay and Edith. When each finds out about the other, they stop seeing him. Moral: You can't have your Kay and Edith too. [127]

• • •

A terrible flood devastates a valley and a man is sitting on top of his house, which is floating down the swollen river. A rescue boat comes near and the man says, "Who are you?"

[PG]RATED

A call from the boat says, "We're from the Red Cross."

The man says, "Sorry, I gave at the office." [132]

• • •

An out of work actor in California got a call from his agent telling him that an actor in a New York play had been injured and couldn't go on and that he arranged for him to take his place.
The actor says, "Great when does the play open?"

The agent says, "Tomorrow."

The actor says, "I'll never be able to learn the lines."

The agent says, "No problem; you just have one line: 'Hark I hear the cannons roar.'"

The actor says, "OK" and gets on the red eye. All night long he practices his one line, "Hark I hear the cannons roar, Hark I hear the cannons roar."

He gets to New York; they put him in his costume, put on his makeup and shove him on stage. Just as he gets on stage he hears this big BOOM.

The actor turns to the actor next to him and says, "What the fuck was that?" [156]

• • •

A man wanted to be the first man to jump off the Empire State Building and survive. As he passed the 50th floor he said, "Well, so far so good." [165]

• • •

A hearse loses its brakes and rolls down a steep hill and crashes into a drug store. The druggist rushes over and says,

PG RATED

"Is there anything I can do to help? The corpse rises up and says, "Is there anything you can do to stop this goddamn coffin?" [174]

• • •

A guy from L.A. asks a New Yorker why all New Yorkers answer a question with a question. The New Yorker says, "What's wrong with that?" [179]

• • •

A man may not be as good as he once was, but once he's as good as he ever was. [408]

• • •

Do you know it's illegal in California to transport seagulls over the state lions for immoral porpoises? [514]

• • •

How many psychiatrists does it take to change a light bulb? Just one, but the bulb has to want to change. [541]

• • •

Know the difference between a snow man and a snow woman? Snow balls. [544]

• • •

Know what the girl mushroom said to the boy mushroom? "You're a fun guy." [649]

• • •

What do you call a cow that has just given birth? Decaffeinated. [650]

• • •

A man goes into an Irish pub and asks for a cup of coffee. The man says, "Without cream."

PG RATED

The waitress says, "We don't have any cream. I'm sorry you'll have to have it without milk." [657]

• • •

Son visits his father at the old folk's home. The son says, "How do you like it here?"

The father leans to his left, but an attendant straightens him up and puts a pillow at his left side. The old man leans to his right, but the attendant straightens him up and puts a pillow on his right side. The father doesn't answer again.

The son says, "How do you like it here?"

The father says, "It's fine, except they don't let you fart." [685]

• • •

Remember the old saying, "Abscess makes a fart go Honda?" [686]

• • •

Guy at a ball game keeps yelling, "Fred!"

Finally a drunk gets up, turns around, and says, "My name's not Fred." [731]

• • •

A friend sees an 80 year-old who is crying and says, "What's the matter?"

The 80 year-old says, "I've got a 30 year-old wife, . The sex is great, I couldn't be happier."

The friend says, "Then why are you crying?"

The 80 year old says, "I can't remember where I live." [753]

• • •

PG RATED

On a cruise, a woman sees a man at the bar and says, "You look just like my third husband."

The man says, "How many times have you been married?"

The woman says, "Twice." [829]

• • •

Know what MDA stands for? Mothers Against Dyslexia. [835]

• • •

Paranoids Anonymous are having a tough time meeting. The president won't tell them where the meetings are going to be held. [844]

• • •

A Notre Dame fan goes into a bar with his dog to watch the S.C. - Notre Dame football game. Each time S.C. scores, the dog walks around on his hind legs barking. When S.C. wins the dog does back flips.

The bartender says, "What does the dog do when Notre Dame wins?"

The fan says, "I don't know. I've only had the dog 9 years." [856]

• • •

Hear about the Siamese twin who moved to England so his twin could drive? [860]

• • •

I'm sure glad the Pilgrims shot a turkey and not a cat for Thanksgiving. [864]

• • •

Know the difference between yogurt and California? Yogurt has a living culture. [875]

• • •

Two Medicare recipients hit it off. The woman says, "Your place or mine?"

The man says, "Whichever has the fewer steps." [877]

• • •

At his 25th wedding anniversary, the husband was crying. His son asked him why and he said, "After your mother and I had been married for 5 years I wanted to kill your mother but I didn't because my lawyer said I would get 20 years."

The son said, "But why are you crying now?"

The husband said, "I just realized that if I hadn't followed my lawyer's advice I would be a free man today." [883]

• • •

Know the difference between Clinton, Brown, and Fonda? Fonda went to Viet Nam. [897]

• • •

Hear about the issue before the Arkansas Supreme Court? After a divorce, do the husband and wife remain brother and sister? [903]

• • •

A Frenchman, a Scot and a Polack all ended up before St. Peter. All of them were smiling. St. Peter asked why they were smiling.

The Frenchman said, "I was making love to a beautiful woman when I died."

The Scot said, "I just won a golf tournament."

The Polack said, "When I was hit by lightning, I thought someone was taking my picture". [1059]

CHAPTER 12
POLITICS

A lot like whoring, but only the tax paying public gets screwed. Life lessons from politicians and an inside look at how they "really roll."

~-~-~-~-~-~~-~-~

President Ford and his wife have started to use a new contraceptive. When he gets into bed she hands him a stick of gum. [418]

• • •

Carter and Jerry Brown were in purgatory being tested before they were admitted to Heaven. A gorgeous blonde with big tits walked by. When Carter said, "I have lusted for her in my heart," his wings fell off. When he bent over to pick them up, Brown's wings fell off. [456]

• • •

Know what Reagan's favorite candy is? Gumdrops. Know what his favorite vegetable is? Jim Brady. [583]

• • •

John Edwards's only mistake was in not having Teddy drive her home. [768]

• • •

Biden would have withdrawn a week earlier, but he couldn't find a copy of Hart's withdrawal speech. [771]

• • •

A reporter asked Hart/Clinton, "What about the abortion bill?" Hart/Clinton said, "I paid it." [782]

PO|LITICS

• • •

After the Democratic convention, Senator Benson's wife turned to him and said, "You're no Jack Kennedy either." [797]

• • •

Hear about the dumb politician who thought that Roe vs. Wade was an option Washington had before he crossed the Delaware? [821]

• • •

The Pope is in America going to a dinner and is annoyed with his slow driver. He tells his driver to switch places, and the Pope takes off down the freeway at 100 miles an hour. A Catholic policeman stops him, but when he sees who it is, he doesn't give him a ticket. When the cop got back to the station and was asked why he didn't write a ticket, he said, "Because if the Pope is the chauffeur, the guy in back must be pretty important." [886]

• • •

A BMW owner and a Rolls owner were always arguing about which was the best car. The BMW owner called the Rolls owner to brag about the bedroom he put in his car. The Rolls owner said, "You mean you got me out of the shower to tell me that?" [887]

• • •

Heard that Hillary shaved her pussy? It's Clinton's new campaign slogan: No More Bush. [899]

• • •

Know why Clinton is jealous of Ted Kennedy? Because Kennedy's girlfriend is dead. [905]

• • •

POLITICS

Hear that Clinton used to tell his staff to have Flowers on his desk at least twice a week? [908]

• • •

Know why the gays voted for Clinton? They always prefer an asshole to a bush. [917]

• • •

Know why Hillary stopped wearing miniskirts? Because when she crossed her legs you could see her balls. [918]

• • •

Barack Obama is widely known as the greatest President in the history of Iran. [1010]

• • •

Know how Bill and Hillary met? Both were dating the same girl. [1011]

• • •

What's brown, has four legs, and smells like pussy? Bill Clinton's desk. [1041]

• • •

Monica changed her registration from Democratic to Republican. The Democratic party had left a bad taste in her mouth. [1045]

• • •

What is this? [Puff out cheeks.] Monica Lewinsky concealing the evidence. [1049]

CHAPTER 13
RACE

~-~-~~-~-~~-~-~

A black civil rights worker is missing for over a week when he is found in a swamp wrapped with 200 pounds of chain. The sheriff says, "Isn't that just like a n****r to steal more chain than he can carry." [22]

• • •

A black civil rights worker is talking to a Southern Colonel. The black says, "Are you in favor of integration?" The Colonel says no.

The black says, "Are you in favor of segregation?" The Colonel says no.

The black says, "If you're not in favor of integration or segregation what are you in favor of?"

The Colonel says, "Slavery." [42]

• • •

A Jewish groom asks his father what he should do on his wedding night. The father says, "Stick the longest thing you've got in the hairiest thing she's got." So the groom spent the night with his nose in her armpit. [44]

• • •

What has a black eye patch and comes in a white box? Sammy Davis, Jr. [46]

• • •

A black sees a new black Cadillac and asks the salesman, "How much is that beautiful flesh-colored Caddy?" [50]

RA|CE

• • •

Hear about Irish arthritis? That's when your prick gets to Dublin. [58]

• • •

Know the definition of tender love? Two Greeks with hemorrhoids. [67]

• • •

How do you get rid of crabs? Just paint one black and the others will move out. [90]

• • •

Know why Jewish girls don't wear chastity belts? Because Jewish boys eat locks. [103]

• • •

What do a washing machine and the NAACP have in common? Each has a black agitator. [108]

• • •

A black is waterskiing off a posh Mississippi resort and the guests complain. The manager goes to the white man who is driving the boat. The white man says, "Don't worry. You may think he's waterskiing, your guests may think he's waterskiing, the n****r may think he's water-skiing, but actually I'm trolling for alligators." [114]

• • •

Guy takes a Polack up on Mulholland Drive and after getting her bra and pants off says, "Get in the back seat."

The Polish girl said no.

The guy says, "Why?"

The Polish girl said, "I like it up here with you." [116]

• • •

Know the three most dangerous things in the world? A black with a law degree, a Mexican with a driver's license and a queer with a broken tooth. [139]

• • •

A Jewish woman goes to a Cecil B. DeMille-type movie about Christians in pagan Rome. When it was over, she went to the manager's office to complain. The manager said, "Well, are you complaining there were no Jewish martyrs in the scene in the Coliseum?"

The Jew said, "No, I'm complaining about that lion in the corner that is not eating." [145]

• • •

An obese man who has tried everything goes to a weight loss clinic that guaranteed its customers would lose weight. The manager says, "See that pretty girl? We lock you in a maze and you can have her if you catch her." The man finally catches the girl, loses 5 pounds, and screws her.

The next week the man says, "I'm back, lock me in."

The manager does and the customer sees a 250-pound black with a 14' -inch cock who says, "When I catch you I'm going to bugger you." [148]

• • •

Two Jewish women meet in Paris and finally one confides, "You know, I've been in Paris for almost a week and I haven't been to the Louvre."

The other woman says, "Well maybe it's the water." [153]

• • •

RA|CE

Know how to break a Polack's finger? Hit him in the nose. [166]

• • •

A Polack complains to the foreman, "How come you get paid more and I do all the hard work?"

The foreman says, "It's because I'm smarter than you and I'll prove it." So he goes over to a large vertical beam and puts his hand on it and says, "Now hit my hand."

The Polack swings but just at the last moment the foreman pulls his own hand away. In pain but convinced, the Polack goes back to the ditch with a very sore hand and his fellow workers ask, "What happened?"

The Polack said, "The foreman convinced me that he was smarter."

The fellow workers ask how he did that. The Polack says, "Try to hit my hand." (Puts his hand in front of his face) [176]

• • •

Every morning a Greek restaurant owner and a Chinese restaurant owner would start the day by washing off the sidewalks in front of their restaurants. Each morning the Greek would say, "Hey China boy! How you flied lice?" After months of this, the Chinese went to UCRA and took English and diction lessons.

The morning after he graduated, the Chinese was waiting for the Greek. Sure enough, when he came out the Greek said, "Hey China boy! How you flied lice?"

The Chinaman said, "That's fried rice you Gleek plick!" [177]

• • •

RACE

A teacher tells her students that whoever can answer a current events question at class the next day will get a week's vacation. One kid got two golf balls and painted them black. The next morning just before class started the kid rolled the balls up the aisle toward the teacher.

The teacher said, "OK who's the trouble maker with the black balls?"

The kid said, "Al Sharpton. See you next week teach." [178]

• • •

Hear about the black who won an athletic scholarship at the University of Mississippi? Got it in javelin catching. [180]

• • •

An old Italian was on his deathbed. When his sons ask where he hid his money, he was too weak to talk and he just pressed his thumb and forefingers together. He miraculously recovered and his sons asked what he meant by pressing his two fingers together. The old man said, "It means I was too sick to do this." Put left palm to right elbow.) [184]

• • •

In the year 2020 everyone has numbers instead of names. A man meets another man at a party and says, "My name is 12345."

The second man says, "My name is 22222."

The first man says, "That's funny. You don't look Jewish." [186]

• • •

U.S. ships have USS on their bows. British ships have HMS. Italian ships have TMB. Stands for: That's-a Ma Boat. [188]

• • •

RA|CE

To view this "too hot to handle" joke—subscribe to our website www.DadsJokeBook.com. [189]

• • •

Some blacks are playing craps when one black rolled the dice, a third die fell out of his sleeve. The biggest black there hands two dice back to him and says, "Here you are motherfucker, your point is 15." [190]

• • •

What do you call a Polack who marries a n****r? A social climber. [194]

• • •

Why does it take 4 Polacks to put a light bulb in the ceiling? One Polack holds the bulb and the other three Polacks turn the ladder. [195]

• • •

Two Jews buy a theater. After the first week, they only had 10 customers. The first Jew says, "Abbie, do you think we'll make it go?"

Abbie says, "I don't know why not, it's 80% wood." [203]

• • •

Hear about the black who married a Jew? They had a son who was the head janitor at the UCLA Medical Center. [204]

• • •

Hear about the black who called to report a dead body at 150th and Sepulveda? The cop says, "Spell 'Sepulveda.'" The black thinks a minute and says, "Tell you what, I'll drag the body to 150th and Main." [205]

• • •

RA|CE

Polack thought he could start his own low-price whorehouse with a rubber pussy. He took out ads in Polish newspapers. Unfortunately, he had to file for bankruptcy when his first Polack customer ate it. [209]

• • •

Sammy Davis, Jr. went in for a hemorrhoidectomy. The operation was delayed for an hour as they had to roll him in flour to find his asshole. [211]

• • •

Hear about the Polack who fell into a barrel of tits and came out sucking his thumb? [214]

• • •

Jewish boy tells his mother that he married a colored girl. The mother is at first horrified, but then after thinking about it says, "That's all right, we can share her three days a week." [222]

• • •

An Israeli and an Egyptian tank collide in a sandstorm.

The Egyptian jumps out and yells, "I surrender."

The Israeli jumps out and yells, "Whiplash!" [230]

• • •

Know why they serve food at a Polish wedding? To keep the flies off the bride. [232]

• • •

Know how Poland got rid of its n****r problem? They told the Polacks they were good to eat. [233]

• • •

RA|CE

Joseph and an obviously pregnant Mary are on their way to Bethlehem. They meet an Arab on the way who asked what they were going to name the child. Mary said they hadn't decided on a name. The Arab suggested Jesus.

Joseph said, "Hell no. What do you think we are, Puerto Rican?" [234]

• • •

Know why the Israeli wars are so short? They use rented equipment. [235]

• • •

A Japanese businessman saw an eye doctor who asked him if he ever had a cataract. The Japanese man said, "No, I only drive Rincons." [239]

• • •

During the Middle Ages, the Pope was trying to get some volunteers to fight in the Crusades so he summoned all the young Italians to St. Peter's Square. He said, "I'm going to choose 10,000 brave young Italians by dropping 10,000 feathers from my balcony and choosing the ones the feathers land on."

After the feathers were dropped he immediately noticed this strong garlic odor. He turned to a priest and said, "Where is that smell coming from?"

The priest said, "Haven't you ever smelled 50,000 Italians blowing at feathers?" [243]

• • •

Definition of masturbation: Polish karate. [246]

• • •

RA|CE

Colored girl comes from a Mississippi farm to Harlem. Her friend warns her to be careful and not get in trouble or she'll get picked up by the fuzz. The colored girl says, "Oohee, I'll bet that do smart." [248]

• • •

Polack is told by his doctor that his asshole has gone bad and that he needs a new one. The Polack says, "What shall I do?"

The doctor says, "Don't worry this is the age of transplants. When a donor asshole is available, I'll put you in the hospital and we'll do a transplant."

One night the Polack got a call from his doctor who told him to get his ass down to the hospital. When the Polack got there he saw that the donor was a big black who had just died. The operation was a success, but the Polack died two days later.

It seems that the asshole rejected him. [249]

• • •

Know who discovered Poland? The Roto-Rooter man. [255]

• • •

Know what this is? (put both hands in your pocket). A Polack counting to 11. [256]

• • •

A reporter asked a white man who had received the first heart transplant from a black if he had noticed any side effects. The man said, "Yes, my cock had grown 6" and I have received 12 welfare checks." [259]

• • •

Two colored men visit the Vatican and see how the Pope lives in a Palace, wears gold shoes, and gets carried around wherever he goes. They ask one of the Swiss Guards, "How do you get to be Pope?"

RA|CE

The guard says, "You get elected by the Cardinals."

One black says to the other, "I wonder why the Giants didn't do something like this for Willie Mays?" [261]

• • •

Two Italians are walking down the street. One sees this big tittied young Italian girl and (making a corkscrewing gesture up) says, "Boy, would I like to fuck that broad."

The second Italian says, "That's-a ma wife." The first Italian (making a corkscrewing gesture down) says, "Scusa Luigi." [272]

• • •

Polack and a Frenchman are hunting and they come to this grassy meadow where they see a beautiful nude woman sunbathing. The Frenchman says, "That looks good enough to eat."

The Polack says "Really?" (Raise rifle and say "bang") [273]

• • •

Paddy died and his friends came to the wake. If anyone asked what Paddy died of, the wife said gonorrhea. When all the guests had left, the eldest son who had been standing next to her in the reception line said, "Mother why did you say Paddy died of gonorrhea? You know he died of diarrhea."

She said, "I know my son but I would rather they remembered him as a sport rather than the shit that he was." [277]

• • •

Jackie bumped into Rose Kennedy and Rose said, "Where have you been?" Jackie said, "I've been in bed with Multiple Sclerosis." Rose said, "I thought I told you to stop running around with that Goddamned Greek." [280]

RA|CE

• • •

Know why Polacks wear turtle neck sweaters? To hide their flea collars. [281]

• • •

A young Polish kid comes home with his report card. The father sees that he got 5 Fs and a D. The father says, "How do you explain this?"

The kid says, "I guess I concentrated too much on one course." [283]

• • •

A man gets really drunk. He wakes up the next morning in a strange hotel room between a real skinny black girl and a 300 pound black woman. He figures he can't sneak out by climbing over the 300 pound black, so he starts to crawl over the skinny one. She wakes up and says, "Oh no, not me, boss. I'm the bridesmaid." [284]

• • •

Black kid kicks a bottle in an alley. It breaks open and a genie pops out and says he can have three wishes. The kid says, "I want to be all white, up tight and out of sight."

The genie says, "Alla Kazam you're a tampon." [303]

• • •

At a newly-integrated school the white kids gave their teacher a birthday cake with the initials "TOT" on it. The black children gave her a cake with "FUCK" on it.

The teacher asked the white kids what TOT meant and they said, "To our teacher."

The teacher asked the black kids what the initials on their cake meant. They said, "From us colored kids." [306]

RA|CE

• • •

How to tell when a Polack is menstruating? When she's only wearing one sweat sock. [310]

• • •

How does a Mexican know when he's hungry? When his asshole stops burning. [317]

• • •

A Jew is down on his luck and goes to a whorehouse. The madam says, "The minimum is $1 for a n****r whore." The Jew finally talks the madam into screwing him for all he has 85 cents.

Fifteen years later he comes back to the same whorehouse a millionaire. He says to the madam, "Do you remember me?"

The madam says, "Yes you're the one who got me pregnant. Meet your son."

The son comes out and groans and says to his mother, "You mean I'm part Jewish?"

The Jew says, "Shut up, you little bastard, if I'd had 15 cents more you'd have been a n****r." [319]

• • •

Jewish woman goes to her psychiatrist complaining about sex. The psychiatrist has her lie nude on his couch for an hour and think about nothing but sex. When the hour is over the psychiatrist says, "What do you think about sex now?"

The woman says, "I still think Saks is the finest store in Beverly Hills." [322]

• • •

Two Polish women go to the butcher shop and want to buy two Polish sausages. The butcher says, "They only come in packages of three."

RA CE

The Polacks argue with the butcher for a while until one says, "Oh what the hell, let's buy three, we can always eat one." [323]

• • •

A guy says, "I saw a n****r with a white cock."

His friend says, "That's just a Polack coal miner on his honeymoon." [328]

• • •

Know what this is? [Put fingers in ears and stomp on ground] A Polack mine detector. [333]

• • •

A Polish regiment declared war on rats. Half defected and the other half brought back war brides. [334]

• • •

An Irishman who worked at a Guinness brewery drowned in a vat of beer. The foreman went to his home to break the news to his wife. The wife started to scream about what a terrible place Guinness was and how poor Paddy never had a chance.

The foreman said, 'No, Paddy had at least two chances."

The widow said, "What do you mean?"

The foreman said, "Well Paddy did climb out twice to take a leak." [337]

• • •

Hear about the Polish parachute? It opens on impact. [340]

• • •

To view this "too hot to handle" joke—subscribe to our website www.DadsJokeBook.com. [344]

• • •

RA|CE

A woman is horrified to learn that her husband promised the child's Polish godfather that he could name the child. She had a girl and the Polack named her Denise. The woman thought that was a pretty name but said, "What would you have named the child if it had been a boy?"

The Polack said, "Da-nephew." [346]

• • •

Know why Polish ballerinas don't do splits? Because they stick to the floor. [349]

• • •

Know what an Obama Fried Chicken Barrel is? It's full of left wings and assholes. [350]

• • •

Polack's on his way to Vegas to get married. He puts his hand on his fiancée's knee. She says, "You can go further if you want to." He says OK and drives to Salt Lake City. [351]

• • •

Ever see Polish Peeping Tom? (Look down at your fly) [354]

• • •

Hear about the Polish grandmother who started taking the pill because she didn't want any more grandchildren? [355]

• • •

Hear about the Polish girl who had two chances to get pregnant and blew both of them? [356]

• • •

If see a white in a white Cadillac, that's White Power. If see a black in a black Cadillac that's Black Power. What is it if you see a Mexican in a brown Cadillac? Grand Theft Auto. [360]

• • •

RA│CE

Scientists have developed a new fish that can live in the Monongahela River. It's called the Kowalski. The only trouble is that it can't swim. [362]

• • •

Know why semen is white and urine is yellow? So Polacks will know if they are coming or going. [364]

• • •

Know what a Polish blind date is? (Cover eyes and jack off) [367]

• • •

Polack was asked to read the bottom line of an eye chart. He says, "Read it? Hell, I know him!" [375]

• • •

Hear about the Polack who traded his wife in on an outhouse? The hole was smaller and it smelled better. [376]

• • •

Hear about the Polish godfather who makes you an offer you can't understand? [378]

• • •

Hear about the Polack who only smelled bad on his left side? He couldn't find any Left Guard. [380]

• • •

Hear that the Russians spent 1 billion rubles on sex research and concluded that a man's penis was shaped so as to satisfy a woman? The U.S. spent billions of dollars and concluded that a man's penis was shaped that way to satisfy the man. The Polish government spent 50 zlotys and concluded a man's penis was shaped that way so your hand wouldn't slip off the end. [382]

• • •

RA|CE

An Israeli is in the US for the first time and tries to strike up a conversation with a New Yorker. The Israeli says, "Don't you think that Netanyahu is doing a good job in Israel?"

The New Yorker says, "Fuck Netanyahu."

This angers the Israeli and he says, "Are you Irish?"

The New Yorker says, "Yes."

The Israeli says, "Fuck Ella Fitzgerald." [383]

• • •

A wealthy Indian bought the California Yacht Club. This was so his son could be the first red son in the sail set. [384]

• • •

Polack gets in the back seat of his car with his girlfriend. He starts to kiss her breasts and she gets so excited she says, "Kiss me where it smells." The Polack says OK, gets in the front seat, and drives her to San Pedro. [385]

• • •

Polack wanted to be buried at sea. His two sons died trying to dig his grave. [389]

• • •

A Jewish man comes back from Palm Springs and a friend asks where he has been. The Jewish man says, "Pal Um Springs."

His friend says, "It's pronounced Palm Springs."

The Jewish man says, "Oh I'm sorry I got it mixed up with Pal Um Beach." [390]

• • •

Jewish man retires but his wife dies shortly thereafter. So Sam loses 50 pounds, gets a facelift and a hair piece. He is happily

RACE

driving down the street in his new Mercedes when a truck hits him and kills him. He gets to Heaven and complains to God, "I've lived a good life, gave to the UJA, why did you let this happen to me?"

God said to Sam, "To tell the truth, Sam, I didn't recognize you." [391]

• • •

Two black students got a grant to do research in Africa. The native chiefs wouldn't let them go out with any native girls so they get a female gorilla that they shared. When the grant expired they wanted to take the gorilla back to UCLA. They found out that Air Poland had the most lax security procedures, so they put a pink dress on the gorilla and successfully boarded the plane.

The two Polish pilots looked back at the passengers and one said, "Isn't it terrible, -those two blacks with the nice Polish girl." [392]

• • •

Hear about Evil Kowalski who was killed in his garbage truck trying to jump over 14 motorcycles? [394]

• • •

The coach at Hamtramack High assembles the team and says, "I understand that we have a case of gonorrhea in the locker room."

The fullback, Kowalski, says, "Gee that's great. I was getting tired of Gatorade." [395]

• • •

Hear about the Polack who married a dog? Yeah, it seems he had to. [396]

• • •

RA|CE

Hear about the Polack bank robber who tied up the safe and blew the teller? [401]

• • •

A Polack is in a police rape lineup. When they bring the victim in, the Polack says, "That's the woman, Officer!" [403]

• • •

A traveling salesman met a Polish farmer's daughter. After a little while they went off in the bushes. The Polish girl says, "Do you want a one-hand job, a two-hand job or a two-hand tongue job?

The traveling salesman said, "A two-hand tongue job."

(The Polish girl sticks her thumbs in her ear, wiggles her fingers, and gives him the ---a razzberry.) [411]

• • •

Hear about the Polish abortion clinic? It's so successful that it has a two year waiting list. [412]

• • •

To view this "too hot to handle" joke—subscribe to our website www.DadsJokeBook.com. [413]

• • •

Two blacks are driving a trash truck down the freeway and are stopped by the cops for leaving litter all over the freeway. To avoid getting a ticket, the cops make one of the blacks lie spread eagled on the trash to hold it down. As they drive under an overpass and, one redneck turns to another and says, "Look at that. Somebody threw away a perfectly good n****r." [416]

• • •

Polish sex manual: - 1st step - put it in; 2nd step - pull it out; 3rd step - repeat if necessary. [420]

• • •

Know why Jesus was not Polish? Couldn't find a virgin or 3 wise men. [421]

• • •

Know what this is? [Draw a picture of a tit on a leash.] Two Polack's walking abreast. [422]

• • •

Hear about the Polack who had a penis transplant? The operation went OK but the Polack's right hand rejected it. [423]

• • •

A Polack applies to the FBI. During the interview he is tested and asked who killed Lincoln. The Polack says, "I don't know."

The Interviewer says, "Well you've got to know to work for the FBI."

Later, a friend asks how the interview went. The Polack says, "Great, I'm already working on a big murder case." [431]

• • •

Jewish lady goes to a butcher to buy an L.I. duck. The butcher brings her one and she smells between its legs and says, "That's not an L.I. duck." The butcher brings out another one. Finally after he brings out the 10th duck, the lady smells between its legs and says, "That's an L.I. duck. What took you so long? What kind of butcher are you?"

The butcher says, "I don't know lady You've got me so confused, you tell me." Butcher turns around bends over and spreads his legs.) [432]

• • •

RA|CE

How do you stop 5 blacks from raping a woman? Throw them a basketball. [434]

• • •

Polack hails a cab and says, "Have you got room for a case of beer, 2 large pizzas, and a dozen hot dogs?" The cabby says sure, so the Polack throws up in the back seat of the cab. [436]

• • •

Know why there are no more Texans? The Okies stopped fucking the Mexicans. [438]

• • •

Know why Jewish women miss short putts? Because all their life they have been told 14" inches is this long. (Show 4") inches.] [439]

• • •

Polack comes up to a friend with two hands full of horse shit. He turns to his friend and says, "Do you know I almost stepped in this?" [440]

• • •

A Polack wants to raise chickens so he plants chicken heads in the ground and waters them but nothing grows. He writes to the Department of Agriculture to tell them what has happened and asks if they can help him. The Department of Agriculture writes back and says, "We can't help you unless you send in a soil sample." [441]

• • •

Know why Lincoln freed the slaves? He thought it would be good for basketball. [448]

• • •

RA|CE

An American has a heart attack in Poland and gets a Polish pacemaker. When he gets back, his American doctor asks if he has had any problems. The American says, "It seems OK but every time I get a hard-on the garage door opens." [450]

• • •

An oil wildcatter near the Mexican border had a well blowout and fire. He called up Red Adair who wanted $10,000 per day to put the fire out. All the other well-known firefighters wanted almost as much. He finally accepted an offer from Rojo Rodriguez to put the fire out for a total of $5,000.

About 10 minutes later, a truck full of Mexicans comes roaring down the hill near the burning well, drives right on to the burning well, and all the Mexicans jump out and beat off the fire with their serapes.

As the wildcatter is writing the check he says, "What are you going to do with all this money?"

The Mexican says, "Well, Señor, the first thing I'm going to do is to fix the brakes on that goddamn truck." [451]

• • •

A 50 year old Jew dies and his widow asks the mortician to cut his cock off and to give it to her. She puts the cock in a pot, and puts in a little celery, salt and chicken fat. Her neighbor is watching aghast. She says, "Sadie what are you doing?"

Sadie says, "For 30 years, I ate it his way. Now I'm going to eat it my way." [453]

• • •

Definition of renege: When they make a substitution in a basketball game. [455]

• • •

RA|CE

Hear about the Mexican who married a Polack? They had a son and named him Retardo. [457]

• • •

An Italian regiment was cut off in North Africa. They had little food and hadn't had any laundry service for six months. The Colonel assembled the regiment and said, "I gotta good news. Each of you can have a change of laundry." A great shout goes up. The Colonel says, "Now Luigi, you change with Pasquale. Giuseppe, you change with Renaldo... " [459]

• • •

The safest day on the L.A. freeways is Sunday. The Jews are in Palm Springs. The Catholics are in church. The Protestants are on the golf course. The blacks are in jail and the Mexicans can't get their cars started. [460]

• • •

Did you hear that Idi Amin killed a thousand blacks just to keep up with the Joneses? [461]

• • •

Just when you thought it was safe to go back to Beverly Hills, out comes Jews II. [462]

• • •

A Japanese student brags he knows more American history than the Americans. An American says, "OK who said, 'Fuck the Japs'?"

The Japanese says, "I don't know."

The American says, "Harry Truman, August 1945." [463]

• • •

A n****r, a Jew, and a Mexican each submit bids to build a bridge. The n****r bid $100,000 for materials, $100,000

RA CE

for labor, and $100,000 for himself. The Mexican bid just $200,000. The Jew bid $900,000.

The buyer opened the bids and asked the Jew how he could justify his bid. He said, "$300,000 for you, $300,000 for me and $300,000 for the n****r to build the bridge." [475]

• • •

Hear about the Polish woman who returned a vibrator and when asked why said it chipped her tooth? [476]

• • •

Polish girl complained to the police that she was raped by a Polack. The cop said, "How did you know it was a Polack?"

The girl said, "I had to help him put it in." [477]

• • •

Polack guerrilla fighter throws the pin at the Germans and holds the grenade in his mouth. [478]

• • •

A cop stops Stella Kowalski for drunk driving. She says, "Isn't there anything I can do to avoid getting arrested?"

The cop pulls his fly down and his cock out. Stella says, "I don't want to take the breathalyzer again." [482]

• • •

An American meets the Pope. They hit it off and the American starts to tell the Pope a Polish joke. The Pope says, "Now remember, I'm Polish."

The American says, "That's OK, I'll speak slowly." [489]

• • •

Hear about the Mick who said he only wanted a bottle in front of me but got a frontal lobotomy? [490]

RA|CE

• • •

Know what they would call a Carter and Jackson ticket? Anus and Andy. [491]

• • •

A New York Jewish CPA gets a call at 2:00 a.m. and is asked if he wants to buy an elephant for $700. The Jew says, "Are you crazy, calling me at 2 in the morning to ask if I want to buy an elephant for $700? I live in a small 2 bedroom apartment in Queens, what would I do with an elephant?"

The caller says, "OK. I'll sell you two elephants for $800."

The CPA says, "OK. you've got a deal." [496]

• • •

Know what a J.A.P. 10 is? A J.A.P. 2 with $8 million. [500]

• • •

Know why there are no Mexican organ grinders? Because though you can train the monkey, but you can't train the Mexican. [501]

• • •

A Jewish boy asks his father, "Dad, what's 'ethics'?"

The father says, "Well, you know I've been in business with your uncle Louie for 40 years. Say a blind man comes into the store and gives me a $100 bill thinking it's a $50. I give him change for a fifty. Now ethics is whether I tell your uncle Louie about the extra $50 or not.." [502]

• • •

Polack went to the doctor's office complaining of diarrhea. The doctor said, "When did you first notice you had diarrhea?" The Polack said, "When I took off my bicycle clips." [504]

• • •

RA|CE

Know how to say, "I'm going to stick this bat up your ass" in Hebrew? "Trust me." [508]

• • •

To view this "too hot to handle" joke—subscribe to our website www.DadsJokeBook.com. [510]

• • •

Know who the most popular guy is at a Mexican wedding? The guy with the jumper cables. [518]

• • •

Two Jewish mothers were talking. One said, "You told me you have a daughter married to a lawyer, a doctor and a CPA but I thought you only had one daughter."

The other Jewish mother says, "Yes, I do. So- much joy from only one daughter." [520]

• • •

Know how to kill a Jewish vampire? Drive a Mercedes through his heart. [523]

• • •

Did you hear about the Polish javelin team that won the toss and elected to receive? [525]

• • •

Know how to stop a Jewish girl from fucking? Marry her. [526]

• • •

Know what Jewish foreplay is? Two hours of begging. [527]

• • •

Hear about the new Vietnamese cookbook? How to wok your dog. [529]

RA|CE

• • •

Know the difference between an elephant and a Polish mother-in-law? About 50 pounds. [530]

• • •

Know how a Polack gets into a sleeping bag? He wakes her up. [531]

• • •

Know why there are so many Polish cesareans? Because it's so hard to pull a square head through a round hole. [533]

• • •

Want to hear a Polish marriage proposal? "You're what?" [535]

• • •

Know why it is so hard to get into a Polish girl's panties? Because she carries them in her purse. [536]

• • •

Do you know what gross ignorance is? 144 Polacks. [537]

• • •

Know what they do with retarded pigs? They make Polish sausage. [538]

• • •

A man is blaming the Jews for all the world's problems. He said that the Jews sank the *Titanic*. A Jew protests and says that the *Titanic* was sunk by an iceberg. The man says, "Iceberg, Goldberg, what's the difference?" [542]

• • •

Know why Jesus wasn't born in Mexico? Because they couldn't find three wise men or a virgin. [543]

• • •

RA CE

To view this "too hot to handle" joke—subscribe to our website www.DadsJokeBook.com. [545]

• • •

To view this "too hot to handle" joke—subscribe to our website www.DadsJokeBook.com. [548]

• • •

Know what you call a n****r in a wet suit? Jacques Custodian. [549]

• • •

Hear about the Polish revolutionary who was told to blow up a car? He came back, but said he failed, as he burnt his lips on the exhaust pipe. [550]

• • •

To view this "too hot to handle" joke—subscribe to our website www.DadsJokeBook.com. [551]

• • •

The EEOC now prohibits anyone from calling a Mexican a "Greaser." You may call them "Lubratinos," however. [556]

• • •

To view this "too hot to handle" joke—subscribe to our website www.DadsJokeBook.com. [557]

• • •

To view this "too hot to handle" joke—subscribe to our website www.DadsJokeBook.com. [558]

• • •

Hear about the Jewish student who was lousy in school? In desperation, his parents finally put him in a Catholic school. He got all A's and his parents asked why. The Jewish kid said, "When I saw that Jewish guy on the cross I knew they meant business." [559]

RA|CE

• • •

Know why it takes so long to circumcise an Iraqi? There's no end to those pricks. [563]

• • •

Kareem Abdul-Jabbar goes to Africa and falls in love with a female gorilla. He brings her back to America and buys her clothes and jewelry on Rodeo Drive. A Jew sees her and says, "How come the damn n****rs get all the good-looking Jewish girls?" [565]

• • •

Hear about the Polack singing group? They eat apples and drink Tab. They're called the Moron Tab-n-Apple Choir. [571]

• • •

Know why n****rs don't sleep on the beach? The cats keep covering them up. [573]

• • •

A Polack is complaining to an Italian about the Italians getting all the good looking women.

The Italian takes pity on him and says, "It's simple. When you go to the beach just put a potato in your swimming suit and all the girls will be following you around."
A week later the Polack said all the women ran away from him.

The Italian said, "Show me what you did."

The Polack came out with his swimming suit on.

The Italian says, "You're supposed to put the potato in the front." [574]

• • •

RA CE

Know what you call a Mexican with 12 kids? El Producto. [579]

• • •

Know the identity of the Atlanta killer? It's an alligator disguised as a watermelon. [581]

• • •

Hear they caught the Atlanta killer? He's Son of Sambo. [585]

• • •

Hear the Jewish position on abortion? It's still a fetus until it graduates from Medical School. [586]

• • •

Know how to get a Polish girl pregnant? Come in her armpit and the flies will do the rest. [590]

• • •

The driver's education and sex education programs have been canceled in the Tijuana schools. It seems that the burro died. [593]

• • •

Hear about the Polish girl that sucked her first cock? She spit out feathers for a week. [594]

• • •

Know why there are no black nuns? They can't say mother superior. [595]

• • •

Hear about the Polack whose wife said, "How many times do I have to tell you not to say fuck in front of the c-h-i-l-d-r-e-n"? [597]

• • •

RA CE

Know why Mexicans have big noses? So they can have something to pick during the off-season. [598]

• • •

Know the definition of a n****r? That distinguished colored man who just left the room. [599]

• • •

What do you get when you cross a French whore and a J.A.P.? A girl who sucks credit cards. [600]

• • •

What's a cacoon? A Na N****r. [602]

• • •

What do you get when you cross Bo Derek and Sammy Davis, Jr.? A 10 of Spades. [603]

• • •

What do you get when you cross an Irishman and a n****r? A lepracoon. [604]

• • •

What do you call a n****r on a white horse? Leroy Rogers. [605]

• • •

Polack attends a spiritualists meeting. The speaker asks if anyone in the audience has seen a ghost. Several hands go up. He then asks those with their hands up if they have ever talked to a ghost. A few hands remain. He then asks if anyone has ever had sex with a ghost. Only the Polack's hand remained up. The speaker then asked the Polack to describe his sexual experience with a ghost.

The Polack says, "Ghost? I thought you said goat." [606]

• • •

RA | CE

Know why God created armadillos? So n****rs could eat possum on the half shell. [610]

• • •

Know what a black test tube baby is called? Janitor in a drum. [611]

• • •

Know how many pallbearers there are at a n****r funeral? Six to carry the casket and one to carry the boombox. [612]

• • •

What's a Watts piñata? A watermelon stuffed with food stamps. [613]

• • •

Know what Polack/Italian foreplay is? (Snap fingers and point at your cock.) [614]

• • •

If Spaniards aren't Jewish, why do they call their son Saul? [615]

• • •

Two Polacks want to go out on the town but they only have $5. One Polack says, "I know what to do." He goes into a drugstore and comes out with five dollars' worth of Kotex.

The second Polack says, "Why did you buy $5 worth of Kotex?"

The first Polack says, "I heard that with Kotex you can go horseback riding, swimming, and skiing." [616]

• • •

Know why Mexicans don't barbecue? The beans fall through the grate. [621]

• • •

RACE

Know why Kinney's is like the Federal government? Because it's got 100,000 black loafers. [622]

• • •

Did you hear why all the blacks are moving from Plano, Texas to Tye, Texas? Because they would rather be a Tye coon than a Plano n****r. [625]

• • •

Know where Oriental eyes come from? Generations of Oriental males saying, "Not rice again." [629]

• • •

What do you call a J.A.P. on a waterbed? The Dead Sea. [634]

• • •

How can you tell your home has been burglarized by a Polack? Your garbage is missing and your dog's been raped. [636]

• • •

Know the difference between a crucifixion and a circumcision? In a crucifixion you throw the whole Jew away. [639]

• • •

Know the difference between a car tire and a n****r? If you put chains on a n****r he'll sing Ol' Man River. [641]

• • •

Know what a J.A.P. blow job is? (blow on your fingernails) [643]

• • •

To view this "too hot to handle" joke—subscribe to our website www.DadsJokeBook.com. [645]

• • •

Know why they can't hold the Olympics in Mexico anymore? All the Mexicans who can swim or run are in Southern California. [656]

• • •

A black woman goes into a grocery store and snaps her fingers at the clerk. She then touches her head, her tit, her ass, and her crotch. The clerk says, "What's that supposed to mean?"

The woman says, "I want a head of lettuce, a chicken breast, a rump roast, and some Brillo pads." [659]

• • •

To view this "too hot to handle" joke—subscribe to our website www.DadsJokeBook.com. [661]

• • •

Do you know why scientists are starting to use Mexicans instead of rats in experiments? Because they breed faster and there's less an emotional attachment to them. [663]

• • •

Hear about the ad in the *Jerusalem Daily News* in 33 A.D.? It shows Jesus on the ground under a cross with broken nails on the cross. The ad says, "When only the best is good enough, use Goldberg nails." [670]

• • •

Definition of a J.A.P.: A barracuda with nail polish. [671]

• • •

Hear about Richard Pryor and Michael Jackson? They started the Ignited Negro Fund. [673]

• • •

If Tarzan and Jane were Italian, Cheeta would be the other woman. If Tarzan and Jane were Polish, Cheetah would be a gifted child. [678]

• • •

RA CE

What do you say to a Mexican in a coat and tie? "How do you plead?" [687]

• • •

Know how the blacks learned how to break dance? Watching Jews go under the doors of pay toilets. [692]

• • •

A patient was being examined by a Polish proctologist and, after being told his prostate will have to be removed, said he wanted a second opinion, so the Polish proctologist stuck two fingers up his ass. [694]

• • •

Know why Polacks always screw on their backs? Because they always fuck up. [695]

• • •

Jewish American Princess' ideal house: 7,000 sq. ft. but no kitchen or bedroom. [696]

• • •

To view this "too hot to handle" joke—subscribe to our website www.DadsJokeBook.com. [698]

• • •

Know the Union Carbide company song, "Ten little, nine little, eight little Indians … ?" [699]

• • •

Man loses his cock in an accident. The doctor takes him to a freezer and there are cocks anywhere from 6" to 14." The man likes the 14" but says he better talk to his wife. He comes back and says, "My wife likes the 14" cock too, but wants to know if it comes in white." [700]

• • •

RA|CE

Hear about the new Japanese-Jewish restaurant? It's called SoSueMe. [701]

• • •

Hear that Carl Lewis lost his Olympic medals? Both his parents appeared nude in *National Geographic*. [702]

• • •

What do you get when you combine a J.A.P. and an IBM? A computer that won't go down on you. [706]

• • •

Know the two biggest Polish lies? "Your check is in my mouth and I won't come in your mailbox." [709]

• • •

Know what a J.A.P.'s husband wants for his anniversary? A picture of his wife on a milk carton. [714]

• • •

Hear about the new J.A.P. disease? It's called Maids. They die without one. [722]

• • •

What do you call a white guy surrounded by 5 blacks? A victim.

What do you call a white guy surrounded by 5000 blacks? A warden.

What do you call a white guy surrounded by 250,000 blacks? Postmaster General. [727]

• • •

Know what Jesus said to the Polacks on Good Friday? "Play dumb till I get back." [736]

• • •

RA|CE

Hear about the porno J.A.P. video? *Debbie Does Dishes.* [737]

• • •

What do you call an Ethiopian with a yeast infection? A quarter pounder with cheese. [741]

• • •

What do you call this? (Hold a black comb upside down.) A bunch of Ethiopians carrying a canoe to a river. [742]

• • •

When does a Mexican become a Spaniard? When he marries your daughter. [744]

• • •

To view this "too hot to handle" joke—subscribe to our website www.DadsJokeBook.com. [748]

• • •

What do you call a black Mormon? A n****r with a garage full of groceries. [754]

• • •

Know the difference between a J.A.P. and Jell-O? Jell-O moves when you eat it. [757]

• • •

Hear about the two Mexicans on *That's Incredible*? One was an only child and the other had car insurance. [758]

• • •

Hear about the Poles who are wearing condoms on their ears? They are trying to avoid getting hearing aids. [762]

• • •

Hear about the guy who won a $1 million dollars in the Polish lottery? He gets a $1 per year for a million years. [765]

• • •

A social worker warned two Polish drug addicts about sharing a needle. One Polack said, "Don't worry, we're wearing condoms." [766]

• • •

A plantation owner wanted to save on labor costs so he bought 10 new cotton-picking machines. The glare from the machines got in motorists' eyes, so after the CHP complained, he painted them black. The next day four didn't show up for work and the rest signed up for welfare. [767]

• • •

Know what you call a watermelon in Chinese? Coon chow. [769]

• • •

Polack offers to buy a woman a drink, but she says, "Don't bother, I'm a lesbian." The Polack says, "What's a lesbian?" The woman says, "See that blonde over there, well I want to rip her clothes off and kiss her tits and pussy." The Polack says, "Gee, I must be a lesbian too." [772]

• • •

Know the difference between a Jew and a pizza? The pizza doesn't scream when you put it in the oven. [778]

• • •

Hear that Victoria Station opened a restaurant in Beverly Hills? It folded in a short time, they couldn't get the Jews into the boxcars. [779]

• • •

Know the difference between an Irish wedding and an Irish wake? One less drunk. [780]

• • •

RA|CE

Know what is black and brown and looks good on a n****r? A Doberman pincher. [791]

• • •

Know what Ben Johnson said after the Olympics? "I didn't take no stereos." [795]

• • •

Greg Louganis lost his medals. They found traces of Ben Johnson in him. [796]

• • •

President Reagan, Al Sharpton, a priest, and a boy scout are on a plane that is about to crash, but there are only three parachutes. President Reagan says, "I'm the president," so he takes a parachute and jumps.

Sharpton says, "I'm the world's smartest n****r," so he takes a parachute and jumps.

The priest turns to the Boy Scout and says, "I've lived my life---You take the last parachute."

The Boy Scout says, "That won't be necessary as the world's smartest n****r just took my knapsack." [798]

• • •

Jew tries to try to get into an L.A. country club. When asked his name he says, "Sam Goldberg."

"What is your business?"

He says, "Women's ready-to-wear."

"What is your religion?"

"Jewish."

RA|CE

He gets a letter two week later saying, "Sorry, but we have no opening for a man with your qualifications."

He complains to a friend who says, "You can't get into L.A.C.C. as a Jew. You have to be a wealthy WASP." So 6 months later, he applies.

"What is your name?"

"Wellington St. John III."

"What is your business?"

"Industrialist."

"What is your religion?"

He says, "Goy." [799]

• • •

Briscoe says he's half Jewish and half Irish. He's the first Jew who didn't want to be 51% of anything. [801]

• • •

How do you say "quicksand" to four Mexicans? "Quatro cinco." Know how you say "co-signer"? "Dos Equis." [813]

• • •

In San Francisco, they put the pictures of missing gays on Vaseline jars, but it's a picture of the back of their head. [814]

• • •

A black came into a bar with a parrot on his shoulder. The bartender says, "Where did you get him?"

The parrot said, "Africa. There's millions of them over there." [816]

• • •

RA|CE

Why were there only 50 Mexicans at the Cinco de Mayo parade? They only had two cars. [817]

• • •

With a Jewish American Princess, the orgasm is fake but the jewelry is real. With a Mexican, the orgasm is real but the jewelry is fake. [824]

• • •

Hear that hurricane Hugo hit Poland and did $200,000,000 in improvements? [825]

• • •

To view this "too hot to handle" joke—subscribe to our website www.DadsJokeBook.com. [831]

• • •

Know what Abe Lincoln said after his first hangover? "I freed who?" [841]

• • •

A pollster asked an Ethiopian, "Pardon me, what is your opinion on the world food shortage?"

The Ethiopian said, "What's food?"

The American said, "What's a shortage?"

The Russian said, "What's an opinion?"

The Jew said, "What's pardon me?" [843]

• • •

To view this "too hot to handle" joke—subscribe to our website www.DadsJokeBook.com. [846]

• • •

RA|CE

Hear about the Jewish child molester? He says, "Hey little girl, want to buy some candy?" [850]

• • •

Man watched a Polish girl take off her pants and start to eat a piece of watermelon. He asked her why she was eating watermelon with her pants off. The Polack said, "It keeps the flies off the watermelon." [854]

• • •

Know the difference between an Iraqi woman and an N.F.L. guard? After 4 periods the guard takes a shower. [857]

• • •

Hear the Iraqis found a new use for sheep? Wool. [858]

• • •

Know why alligators are like Italians? The both have short legs and they make good shoes. [863]

• • •

A Southern cop crashes into two blacks and one comes through the windshield. The second cop says, "What will we do?"

The first cop says, "We can arrest the one that came through the windshield with breaking and entering and we can drop the other off in a corn field and arrest him for leaving the scene of a crime." [866]

• • •

A Polack has been in high school for 6 years. His father is a powerful local politician so the principal agrees he can graduate if he passes a test. All the Polacks attend the graduation ceremony and the principal says, "Mr. Kowalski what is 6 plus 9?"

RA|CE

The Polack takes off one shoe and after five minutes looks up and says, "15?"

The Polish audience jumps up and as one says, "Hey, give the boy another chance." [870]

• • •

Two Irishmen slowly start across a narrow country road on a tractor, oblivious to any traffic. A sports car comes around the bend and to avoid the tractor, turns into the pasture fence, rips across 200 feet of pasture and swerves back on the road. The tractor driver turns to his friend and says, "Mother of God, Patrick, we got out of that pasture just in time." [885]

• • •

Know why a black's eyes are red after intercourse? Mace. [913]

• • •

Why is Rodney King like David Koresh? They're both black. [915]

• • •

Hillary comes up to Bill and says, "I don't really want to go to the D-Day celebration."

Bill says, "I can get you out of it if you give me a blow job."

Hillary goes down on him and says, "Your dick tastes like shit."

Bill says, "Yeah, Al didn't want to go, either." [922]

• • •

Hear about the Polish man who said to his wife, "Send the kids outside to p-l-a-y, so we can fuck." [923]

• • •

A Polack and an Italian were hired to install telephone poles. At the end of the day the foreman asked the Italian how many

RA|CE

telephone poles he had installed. The Italian said 12. The foreman asked the Polack the same question. The Polack said 2. The foreman said, "How come you only installed 2 and Luigi installed 12?"

The Polack said, "Well, look how far his poles stick out of the ground." [925]

• • •

How do you set up a [Polish/Black/Mexican] guy in a small business? Set him up in a large business and wait. [930]

• • •

A Jewish girl asks her father for $50. The father says, "$40, what do you need $30 for?" [931]

• • •

A Jew, a black, and a redneck helped free a genie from a large buried urn, so the genie gave each of them one wish.

The Jew said, "I wish all Jews were happy and in Israel." The genie said, "Done."

The black said, "I wish all blacks were happy and in Africa." The genie said, "Done."

The redneck said, "You mean all the Jews are now in Israel and all the blacks are in Africa?"

The genie said, "Yes."

The redneck said, "You got a cold Lone Star beer?" [934]

• • •

An Irishman left Ireland for England and got a job with a wealthy Englishman living outside London. The Englishman said, "Well your first job will be to take this redwood stain and paint my porch." About three hours later, the Irishman came

RA|CE

back and said, "I finished the job sir, but that's a Mercedes not a Porsche." [937]

• • •

Lifeguard saves a Jewish man from drowning in Miami Beach. When he gets the Jewish man close to shore he says, "Can you float alone?" The Jewish man says, "Thank you for saving my life, but is this a good time to talk business?" [948]

• • •

A guy who owns a sex store asks his friend to watch the shop while he goes to a doctor's appointment. The owner explains where everything is and leaves. About a half an hour later a white woman comes in and says, "Do you have any vibrators?"

The man says, "Yes, in this display window here."

The woman says, "I'll take the white one."

Twenty minutes goes by and a black woman comes in and says, "Have you got any vibrators?"

The man says, "Yes, in this display window here."

The black woman says, "I'll take the black one."

Another twenty minutes goes by and a Scottish woman comes in and says, "Do you have any vibrators?"

The man says, "Yes, in this display window here."

The Scottish woman says, "I'll take the plaid one."

An hour goes by and the owner returns and says, "How did things go?"

The man said, "Great. I sold two vibrators and my thermos." [954]

• • •

A Jewish man met a gentile in college and became friends. The Jew asks the gentile to go to a bar mitzvah with him. While they are standing around with drinks in their hands, the Jew says, "You seem very nervous and concerned."

The gentile says, "Yes I am. I'm 21 years old and tomorrow I'm going to get circumcised."

The Jew says, "Well you should be concerned. After I had mine, I couldn't walk for 18 months." [955]

• • •

A wealthy older man had an estate in Ireland. He hired a beautiful young Irish girl as a maid. One thing led to another and she became pregnant. When the girl's father found out he went to the Englishman's estate complaining bitterly about how he was going to explain this to the families priest and that this was the first time such a thing had happened in his family. He then asked the Englishman what he was going to do about it. The Englishman acknowledged he had gotten the girl pregnant and said that if she had a girl, he would give her 100,000 pounds and an apartment in Dublin. He then said if she had a boy he would give her 200,000 pounds and the large estate next to his. Then he wondered, what he should do if she had a miscarriage. The father thought a minute and said, "Well, you'll just have to fook her again." [983]

• • •

A Mormon boy and an Irish boy were taking their first airplane flight. The stewardess came down the aisle with the drinks tray and asked the Irish boy if he would like a drink.

He said, "I would like a Scotch and water." She gave him the drink and asked the Mormon boy if he would like a drink.

RACE

The Mormon boy said, "I would rather be raped by 12 sex starved beautiful women than let liquor touch my lips."

The Irish kid handed his drink back to the stewardess and said, "So would I, I didn't know I had that choice" [984]

• • •

O'Reilly comes into the pub all beat up around the head and his right arm in a sling. The bartender says, "Mother of God! What happened to you?"

O'Reilly says, "I got into a fight with O'Brien."

The bartender says, "You outweigh him by 4 stone. He must have had something in his hand."

O'Reilly says, "Aye he did, a shovel, and he beat me with it somethin' terrible."

The bartender says, "Didn't you have anything in your hand?"

O'Reilly says "Aye, Mrs. O'Brien's left breast, a thing of great beauty, but useless in a fight." [985]

• • •

Pat Murphy steps off the bus on his first day in England and walks down Bond Street. Inside the shop are two snobbish Englishmen who have brought in boxes containing all the clothes they are going to sell in a very exclusive bespoke clothing store. They are tired and sitting on the boxes when Murphy walks in and says, "Faith an' what be you selling?"

One of the Englishmen, knowing Murphy won't be able to buy their clothes says, "Assholes."

Murphy looks at them and says, "Well, business must be good, I see you've only got two left." [987]

• • •

RA|CE

An immigrant fresh from Ireland is walking down Bond Street for the first time and sees a window advertising suits for 5 pounds, pants for 2 pounds, and dresses for 7 pounds. He figures he could buy them and take them back to Dublin and make a fortune. He goes into the shop and says, "I want ten suits, 20 pairs of pants, and a dozen dresses."

The attendant says, "Sir this is a dry-cleaning establishment." [996]

• • •

A Jewish man named Goldberg had a store in an Irish neighborhood. He wanted to change his name to an Irish name, so he went to court and asked the judge to change his name to O'Brian. The judge asked why.

Mr. Goldberg said, "I have a shop in an Irish neighborhood and an Irish name would help my business."

The judge said, "Motion granted."

About six months later, he went before the same judge and asked to change his name to O'Reilly.

The judge said, "Didn't you come before this court about six months ago to change your name to O'Brian?"

The Jewish man said, "Yes, your Honor."

The judge said, "Why do you now want to change your name to O'Reilly?"

The Jewish man said, "So when I am asked what my name was before O'Reilly, I can say my name was O'Brian." [1002]

• • •

Where do cocoons come from? Ca-compton. [1006]

• • •

RA|CE

Japanese girls are so tight that when they queef they break glass. [1007]

• • •

What would the Beatles have been called if they were blacks? N****rs. [1015]

• • •

A Jewish child comes home from school. His mother says, "Did you get a part in the school play?"

The boy says, "Yes, I play the part of a Jewish husband."

The mother says, "You go back to that teacher and demand a speaking role!" [1022]

• • •

Know when a Jewish man stops masturbating? When his wife dies. [1028]

• • •

Know why Jews play porno films backwards? They like to see the whore give the money back. [1053]

• • •

The owner of a Chinese restaurant goes on his honeymoon with his wife and when they go to bed he asks her what she would like. His wife says, "How about a 69?"

The husband says, "You want shrimp with lobster sauce?" [1056]

• • •

A woman goes to the doctor and says, "I hurt every time I touch myself."

The doctor says, "You're Polish, aren't you?"

RA|CE

The woman says, "Yes, how did you know?"

The doctor says, "You have a broken finger." [1060]

CHAPTER 14
RELIGION

Help start wars in your country with these charming jokes about priests, rabbis, and the devout. While their overall contribution to SEX has gone down lately, we must reflect on the worldwide benefits of their missionary zeal.

~-~-~~-~-~-~~-~-~

A rabbi prays to God complaining, "What should I do? My son doesn't want to follow in my footsteps. He wants to start a new religion."

A loud voice from Heaven says, "Strange that you should mention it ... " [15]

• • •

A black wants to desegregate a local all-white Baptist church. He is told that to become a member he must undergo baptism by the total immersion method. He dies and goes to Heaven. St. Peter asks him what happened. The black says, "I was being baptized by the total immersion method and that's the last thing I remember." [23]

• • •

As the lawyer told Mary, "I don't care what the angels told you, you are in deep trouble." [31]

• • •

Mother Superior sees some nuns in bikinis. Confused, flustered, and shocked, she runs over to the nuns and says, "If St. Finger saw you, he'd shake his peter at you." [118]

• • •

RELIGION

A man went into a confessional and tells the priest that he made love five times last night to a woman to whom he was not married. The priest said, "As a penance you'll have to say 100 Hail Marys."

The man says, "What's a Hail Mary?"

The priest said, "Aren't you a Catholic?"

"No."The man said no.

The Priest said, "Then why are you here?"

The man said, "Well I'm a stranger in town and I just had to tell somebody." [129]

• • •

A minister was doing badly in getting contributions and increasing attendance. He learns hypnotism and started preaching in a monotone, swinging his watch on a watchchain. He asked for more frequent attendance and for more $20.00 contributions. Attendance and contributions soared. However, one Sunday while the minister was preaching, the watch chain broke and the minister said, "Shit."

Do you know it took almost a week to clean that church out? [133]

• • •

In one section of New York there was a wealthy Jewish synagogue but the local Catholic Church was dirt poor. One day, the rabbi tells his wife that in response to a request from a priest, he just paid for a new urinal in the Catholic Church.

The wife says, "What's a urinal?"

The rabbi says, "How should I know? I'm not a Catholic." [155]

[RE]LIGION

• • •

A visiting priest goes down to the restaurant in the hotel and zeros in on the check girl. He finally talks her into going to bed with him saying, "The good book says it's OK."

When it's over, she says, "OK, show me where in the good book it says we could have sex."

The priest gets out the Gideon Bible and shows her the flyleaf where someone had written, "Screw the hat-check girl. She's the best fuck in town." [157]

• • •

A girl shows up at the Pearly Gates and St. Peter says, "Were you married?" The girl says no.

St. Peter says, "Well, you're going to have to prove you were a virgin to get in." After the examination, St. Peter says, "Well it appears you were a virgin. Your hymen isn't broken, but it has 7 dents in it. What's your name?"

The girl says, "Snow White." [158]

• • •

A black was asking a rabbi about becoming a Jew, and during the discussion the rabbi talked about the Jewish holidays and mentioned that on Jewish holidays they always blew the shofur. When a black friend asked what he was told by the rabbi, the black said that it was looking good. "Those Jews really know how to take care of us colored folks." [159]

• • •

A bum developed an eerie resemblance to Jesus. He finally went into a Catholic church, proclaimed himself Jesus and said, "I've come to collect the rent on the house of God." The priest genuflected and gave him all the money that had been collected.

RE|LIGION

The bum then went to a Protestant church, said the same thing, and got all their collections.

Walking by a synagogue, he walked in and said, "I'm Jesus and I've come to collect the rent on the house of God."

The rabbi yelled to two members, "There's that guy again! Get the 2 x 4s and nails." [160]

• • •

A priest was vacationing on the Riviera and decided to approach a young girl with big tits in a bikini. When he approached her, she said, "Hello, Father O'Reilly."

He said, "How did you know I'm a priest?"

She said, "Don't you recognize me? I'm Sister Margaret." [161]

• • •

At the Pearly Gates, a man sees two gates: One marked for men who are not dominated by their wives, the other for men dominated by their wives. There was only one man in the line for men not dominated by their wives.

St. Peter says, "Why are you in this line?"

The man says, "My wife told me to stand here." [164]

• • •

LBJ calls up the Pope and, after a little small talk, asks if he could make Martin Luther King a Bishop. The Pope said he would think about it but "Why do you want him to be a Bishop?"

LBJ says, "Then I'll only have to kiss his ring." [171]

• • •

Jesus is standing in front of an angry mob which is armed with

RE|LIGION

rocks. He puts his hand up and says, "Let those among you who are without sin cast the first stone." He turns his head and is hit in the back of the ear with a rock. He turns to see who threw it and says, "Mother, I told you to stay out of this." [198]

• • •

Jesus is being put up on the cross. A Roman soldier starts to pound in the first nail. Jesus says, "Would he believe 'Prince of the Jews'?" [199]

• • •

God is thinking about a vacation and one of his angels suggests going to Earth. God says, "No, I went there about 2,000 years ago and got a little Jewish girl pregnant and I've had nothing but trouble ever since." [219]

• • •

A Rabbi in a small Polish town had a son who wasn't very bright. So the town council gave him the job of standing on top of the highest hill in the town to watch for the Messiah. The son came back after a couple of weeks complaining about the low pay, boring working conditions, and no opportunity for advancement. The Rabbi says, "That's true, but remember, it's a lifetime job." [357]

• • •

The Papal Nuncio runs up to the Pope and says, "Holy Father I have good news and bad news."

The Pope says, "What is the good news?"

The Nuncio says Jesus Christ called and he says he's returned to earth.

The Pope says, "That's marvelous. What could possibly be the bad news?"

The Nuncio says, "He's calling from Salt Lake City." [410]

RE|LIGION

• • •

An American pilot decides to fly for the Egyptian Air Force, which pays $10,000 a month. He is about to take his first flight but he can't find any parachute. The Egyptian instructor says, "You don't need one. If you are in trouble just bail out and yell: 'Allah save me.'"

On his first flight, he is hit by Israeli gunfire so he bails out and yells, "Allah save me." An enormous hand comes out of a cloud and stops his fall. (Gesture.)

The American wipes his brow and says, "Jesus Christ." (The hand turns from palm up to palm down.) [417]

• • •

A minister is hiking, and is lost in thought, planning his next sermon, when he falls. He grabs a small branch which prevents his falling over a 1000 foot cliff. When his grip starts to weaken he yells, "Is there anybody up there?"

A deep voice says, "Yes. Who are you and have you led a good life?"

The man yells back and says, "Yes I'm Pastor Jones and you should have a record of me."

The voice says, "Well, our computer has broken down and we can't find your records, but if you will demonstrate your faith by letting go of that branch you will be saved."

The minister thought about this for a minute and yelled, "Is there anybody else up there?" [419]

• • •

Rabbi was an avid golfer and he prayed and prayed to find out if there was a golf course in Heaven. Finally Moses answered his prayers, saying, "I've got good news and bad news. The good news is there is a terrific golf course in Heaven. " The

RE|LIGION

rabbi says. "What's the bad news?" Moses says, "The bad news is you've got a 9:00 a.m. starting time tomorrow morning." [425]

• • •

A kid goes to school and is worried he'll get a lot of homework. The teacher says, "Don't worry. there won't be any homework. You just have to remember my name. It's Miss Prussy."

He is still worried, but a friend says, "Don't worry--just remember pussy with an 'r.'"

The kid practices all that afternoon saying pussy with an "r." He goes to school the next day and the teacher says who remembers my name. The kid says, "I do."

The teacher says, "OK. What's my name?"

The kid says, "Miss Crunt?" [430]

• • •

A young woman in training to be a nun steps into dog shit and says, "Oh shit." She then says, "Christ, I said 'shit.'" The nun then says, "Goddamn it, I said 'Christ!'" She then says, "Fuck it. I always wanted to be a stewardess anyway." [442]

• • •

Nun had to do some painting so she took her habit off so as not to get any paint on it. Knock on the door. Nun asked, "Who is it?"

The man said, "I'm the blind man."

The sister thought, "Well since he's blind I won't have to put my habit on." So she let him in.

He said, "Sister, you've got a great pair of tits. Now where do you want the blinds installed?" [449]

RE LIGION

• • •

A priest in Hollywood hears a woman confess that she gave a man a blow job. The priest asks his Bishop what a blow job is, but the bishop doesn't know. The Bishop asks the Archbishop, but the Archbishop doesn't know. The Archbishop asks a Cardinal and he doesn't know. The Cardinal tells the problem to the Pope says, "Well I don't know about Hollywood, but in Rome it's about 50,000 lira." [493]

• • •

An American in Rome goes to St. Peter's and stands in a long line. The American is clean and well dressed but the Pope embraces a bum next to him in filthy clothes. The bum goes 200' down the line and the American follows him. The Pope's sedan chair again stops and the Pope embraces the bum again and whispers something in the bum's ear. The American asks the bum what the Pope said. The bum says, "The Pope said, 'I thought I told you to get the fuck out of here.'" [577]

• • •

Pope goes to Heaven and after going through the welcoming ceremonies is given a small hut as his living quarters. He doesn't complain until he finds out that a mile away a lawyer is living in a big mansion. When he complains to St. Peter, St. Peter says, "Well we have lots of Popes in Heaven, but that is our only lawyer." [607]

• • •

A Bishop hears the confession of a priest. The priest says, "I screwed the cat at the monastery." The Bishop says he must change his sinful habits and say 50 Hail Marys. The next week, the Bishop hears the same confession and imposes a penance of 100 Hail Marys.

However, the bishop gets a little horny and, seeing the monastery cat, takes it to his room and tries to screw it. The cat screams, scratches, and bites the Bishop. A chastened

RE|LIGION

Bishop hears the same confession next week and says, "Tell me, my son. how did you screw the monastery cat?"

The priest says, "Well you get a box with two holes and put the cat in it."

The Bishop says, "Go on, my son."

The priest says, "You put the cat's tail in the upper hole, close the box and pull the cat's tail, and screw the cat through the lower hole." [608]

• • •

Through a mix-up, a recently deceased Pope ended up in hell and Bill Clinton ended up in heaven. About half an hour later the mix up was cleared up. When the Pope finally got to heaven, he said the first thing he wanted to do was to meet the Virgin Mary. St. Peter said, "Sorry you're about 30 minutes late." [638]

• • •

Know why Jesus doesn't eat M&Ms? Because they fall through the holes in his hands. [651]

• • •

Know why Kraft is moving its plants to Israel? So they can call their products Cheeses of Nazareth. [652]

• • •

Drunk goes into a confessional. Priest hears drunk groaning and asks, "Can I help you?"

The drunk says, "Yeah, have you got any paper in your booth?" [683]

• • •

Jew meets an American at the Wailing Wall. The American asks, "What are you praying for?"

RE|LIGION

The Jew says, "For my wife to stop spending my money, for my daughter to get married, and for my son to graduate from medical school." The Jew says, " But it's just like hitting my head against a stone wall." [751]

• • •

God is bored. He sees a rower counting out "1-2-3-4." He thinks, "What if I were to remove the right side of his brain?" The rower goes, "2-4-6-8." God thinks, "What if I were to cut out the left side of his brain?" The rower goes, "1-3-5-7." God thinks, "What if I were to cut out both sides of his brain?" The rower goes, "Uno, dos, tres, quatro." [869]

• • •

Three men of the cloth are playing golf behind a very slow foursome. Finally the priest complains to the marshal who comes back and says, "They are playing slowly because they are blind."

The priest says, "I will give my next sermon about overcoming handicaps."

The Protestant minister says, "I will give my next sermon about patience and understanding."

The rabbi says, "Fuck "em. Let 'em play at night." [874]

• • •

A priest volunteered to teach a young girl with big tits how to swim. After about 5 minutes the young girl says to the priest, "Will I really sink if you take your finger out?" [927]

• • •

Two nuns were transferred to Transylvania. They were driving to the Nunnery, when they were slowing for a hairpin curve, Dracula jumped on the hood of their rental car.

RELIGION

The nun in the passenger seat said, "Turn on the windshield washers, it was empty so I put holy water in it."

Dracula moaned in pain when he was hit with the holy water, but hung on.

The passenger nun said, "Remember it's Dracula, show him your cross."

So the nun who was driving rolled down the window and yelled, "Dracula get your big fat ass off of the hood of my fucking car." [947]

• • •

Know the difference between a pimple and a priest? The pimple doesn't come on your face until you're 13. [957]

• • •

The Muslims don't recognize the Jewish religion. The Jewish religion doesn't recognize the Christian religion. The Catholic religion doesn't recognize the Protestant religion and the Baptists don't recognize each other in liquor stores or at Hooters. [959]

• • •

The congregation of a temple gives its favorite rabbi a Hawaiian vacation. One day after swimming; he comes back to his hotel room and sees a beautiful nude woman in his bed. She says, "I'm a gift from your temple."

The rabbi gets on the phone and calls his temple angrily complaining that this is a sin that it will bring ill repute on the temple and that it was a terrible thing to do. When he hangs up the phone, he sees the girl putting her clothes on. The rabbi says, "Where are you going? I'm not mad at you." [972]

• • •

RE|LIGION

The local priest got sick one Sunday morning and there are at least 100 people lined up for confessional. He turns to a young altar boy and says, "You want to be a priest, here is a list of what each person must do to be forgiven for each sin. The older altar boy will be here to help you if you have any questions."

A woman came in and says, "I had sex with my brother-in-law." The altar boy looks on the list and sees that it calls for 100 Hail Marys for adultery." He tells the woman this.

The next person is a man who says, "I stole money from my employer." The altar boy looks up stealing and sees that it calls for 50 Hail Marys. He tells the man this.

The next person is a woman who comes in and says, "I gave my employer a blow job." The altar boy looks on the list and there is no mention of a blow job. He turns to the older altar boy and asks, "What does Father Murphy give for a blow job?"

The older altar boy says, "Three Hershey bars and two bags of gummy bears." [975]

•••

A very devoted Catholic is recently widowed and is lonely. She knows her priest has 2 male parrots and she decides to get 2 female parrots for company. She goes to a pet store and buys 2 female parrots. She brings them home and is horrified to find out that the only thing they will say is, "Hi, we're hookers, do you want to get laid?" She is too embarrassed to go back to the pet store so she related her problem to the priest.

He says, "Bring your parrots over to my place. I have 2 male parrots who I have taught to pray and to use prayer beads. Perhaps their religious background will raise the moral standards of your birds."

So the widow brings her parrots over to the priest's house.

RE|LIGION

Sure enough as soon as she puts her parrot's cage down one of the birds says, "Hi, we're hookers, do you want to get laid?"

One of the male parrots turns to his buddy and says, "Ralph, you can put your beads down, our prayers have been answered." [980]

• • •

A church member asks his pastor for help with his hearing. The pastor places his hands on his shoulders and recounts how Jesus cured the sick and told him that his belief in Jesus would lead to a cure.

The man turned to the pastor and said, "But pastor my hearing isn't until next Wednesday." [995]

• • •

Every morning for the last 5 years, when a Jewish man named Sam walked to Temple on Saturday morning, he prayed that he would win the lottery. This Saturday morning, however, the clouds parted and a voice said, "Sam, this is your God."

Sam said, "Yes God."

God said, "Every morning when you walk to Temple you pray to win the lottery."

Sam said, "Yes God that is true."

God said, "Meet me half way Sam. Buy a ticket." [1001]

• • •

A guy goes into a sex shop to buy an inflatable girlfriend. The clerk asks him if he wants the regular model or the Muslim version. Guy asks what's the difference? The clerk says, "The Muslim dolls blow themselves up." [1008]

• • •

RE|LIGION

Two guys are at the airport. The first guy says I thinks I see Mother Teresa. The second guy says, "Go ask her."

The first guy goes over and asks the woman if she is Mother Teresa. The woman says, "Fuck off, you stupid cocksucker!"

He goes back and the second guy who asks what happened. The first guy says "She wouldn't answer my question. I guess I'll never know". [1013]

• • •

A man is doing a crossword puzzle waiting for the service to begin and he asks his priest if he knows a 4 letter word where the last letters are "unt" The priest says "aunt." The man says, "Father, have you got an eraser?" [1021]

• • •

The Mother Superior takes a nun on a bicycle ride with her. The nun says, "I never came this way before."

The Mother Superior says, "Maybe it's the cobblestones." [1027]

• • •

We live in a strange society. The only people who want to get married are gays and priests. [1037]

CHAPTER 15
RUDE & CRUDE

Really Rude, Really Crude jokes. Need we say more, uh, with our mouths full perhaps?

~ - ~ - ~ ~ - - - ~ ~ - ~ - ~

A woman comes into a talent agent's office and proceeds put a harmonica in her pussy and play it. The agent calls up a producer and puts the phone near her pussy and has her play a song. The agent then asks the producer if he likes the act.

The producer says, "No. It sounds like some old cunt playing the harmonica." [14]

• • •

Mother catches her son jacking off and tells him that if he keeps that up he'll go blind. The son thinks a minute and says, "Is it OK if I do it just until I just need glasses." [33]

• • •

Two cannibals agree to share a victim by each starting to eat at opposite ends. Soon after they start eating one says to the other, "How are you doing?"

The other says, "I'm having a ball."

The first says, "You're eating too fast." [43]

• • •

Know what a French luau is? It's where you eat the women and fuck the pigs. [53]

• • •

Ever see a one-eyed sex fiend? (Close one eye.) [57]

⋯

Know what has four balls and eats ants? Two uncles. [59]

⋯

Know how to make a broad jump? [Lick up with tongue.] [64]

⋯

Know what they use a pussy stretcher for? To take a sick pussy to the hospital. [70]

⋯

A man is going down on a woman for the first time and says, "God you have a big pussy. God you have a big pussy."

The woman says, "I know but you don't have to say it twice."

The man says, "I only said it once." [131]

⋯

A man ate at a restaurant for 25 years and always had the same thing, chicken soup. One day while having lunch he notices a hair in his soup and calls the manager over to complain. The manager tried tries to calm him down by saying that, for example, if he was were at a whorehouse eating a pussy he wouldn't complain about a hair in his mouth.

The man said, "You're right, but I sure as hell would complain about a noodle in the pussy." [154]

⋯

A purchasing agent was promised four big titted girls for placing an order with a company. The agent went to the drug store and asked the druggist for a pill which would keep him hard and horny for hours. The next day and he asked for some liniment for soreness.

The druggist said, "Is it for your cock?"

RUDE & CRUDE

The agent said, "No, it's for my right arm. Those damn girls never showed up." [168]

• • •

A middle-aged man goes to a urologist complaining about his cock dribbling every time he goes to the john. The urologist says, "Well we have a new operation for that which requires we transplant a nose hair to the end of your cock."

The man says, "What good will that do?"

The doctor says, "After you finish peeing, you shake your cock and then go [sniff]." [187]

• • •

Guy meets a good looking girl at a bar and after a couple of drinks asks her over to his apartment. She says, "No, I'm on my menstrual cycle.

The guy says, "That's OK. I'll follow you on my Honda." [201]

• • •

World's most disappointed man: Walks into a wall with a hard-on and breaks his nose. [202]

• • •

Do you know how much calcium there is in a kiss? Enough to make a bone about this long [show 7 inches with hands]. [213]

• • •

A guy was having a lot of trouble getting his 1-inch cock out to pee. The guy at the next urinal can't help noticing and says, "Does the small size give you trouble when you're screwing?"

The guy says, "No, then it's twice as big and two people are looking for it." [223]

RUDE & CRUDE

• • •

Guy said, "It's been so long since I've had any, I've forgotten what it tastes like." [228]

• • •

A college student was invited to a very ritzy New Year's Eve party where he got very, very drunk. The next morning he woke up and the only thing he could remember about the apartment he was in was that it had a golden toilet. He asked the doorman if he knew which of the apartments had a golden toilet.

The doorman stepped to the phone and called one of the residents and said, "Mr. Smith, I think I know who crapped in your tuba." [241]

• • •

Man with a wooden eye is upset by all the jokes about his eye so he leaves his small town and goes to New York City. He finally meets a girl there whose mouth runs up and down and not side to side. He falls in love and finally says, "Would you marry me?"

The girl says, "Oh, wouldn't I!"

The guy says, "Well, if you're going to make fun of my wooden eye, fuck you, cunt face." [250]

• • •

A woman goes to her druggist and asks if he has anything to make her pussy smaller. The druggist says sure and gives her some pills. The woman comes back two days later and says, "This doesn't make my pussy smaller. It just makes it open and close."

The druggist looks at the pills and says, "Sorry. I made a mistake and accidentally gave you Chiclets." [257]

RU|DE & CRUDE

• • •

A man with a bladder problem rushes into a ladies' room to pee. A woman sees him and says, "This is just for women."

The man takes his cock out and says, "So is this, but I just want to use it for a minute." [260]

• • •

During a lewd-behavior-and-sexual harassment trial, the complaining witness when asked to repeat the lewd offer said she couldn't, it was too vile. Finally it was agreed she could write it down on a piece of paper. The piece of paper was passed around among the jurors. A female juror tried to pass it to the male juror next to her, but he was asleep. She woke him up and passed him the note. The male juror said, "OK, how about during the noon recess?" [265]

• • •

A woman at a bar asks the man next to her what time it is. He pulls down his zipper and pulls out his cock and says, "9 o'clock."

The woman is a little startled, but says thank you. Some time later, she again asks the man what time it is. He pulls out his cock and says, "9 o'clock."

The woman says, "You told me it was 9 o'clock some time ago."

The man says damn and starts to masturbate and says, "These self-winding watches aren't worth the trouble." [266]

• • •

A man says to a woman, "Would you like to hear a dirty story? It will make you laugh so hard your tits will droop." He looks down at her chest and says, "Sorry, I guess you've already heard it." [271]

• • •

RUDE & CRUDE

A drunk walks into a police station and says he wants to report a stolen car. The cop says, "Where was the car the last time you saw it?"

The drunk says, "Right at the end of this key."

The cop looks down and says, "Do you know your cock is hanging out of your pants?"

The drunk says, "Oh my God. I also want to report a missing girlfriend." [275]

• • •

Man in a 3 piece suit is on a plane reading Playboy. He comes to the centerfold and gets so excited that he puts his tray up, puts his drink on the floor, pulls his cock out, and starts to masturbate. When he's through, he puts his cock back in his pants, pulls down his tray, takes a sip of his drink, pulls out a pack of cigarettes, and turns to the woman next to him and says, "Pardon me. Do you mind if I smoke?" [282]

• • •

Guy talks his girlfriend into a blow job. She gets a mouthful of cum and says, "What do I do now?"

The guy says, "Beats the shit out of me. I'm no cocksucker." [286]

• • •

Two guys were talking about girls. One guy says that he likes to screw girls who smoke. The other guy asks why. [Put one finger in a hole made by his other hand. cough and squeezes that finger at the same time.] [291]

• • •

A flea got a spot in Al Hirt's beard through a rental agency. After a couple of weeks the flea called up the agency and said, "You have to get me a place where there isn't all this loud music."

The agent said, "How about Zsa Zsa's pussy?"

The flea says great and he rides along to a big Hollywood party. The next morning he calls his agent and says, "You have to get me out of here."

The agent says, "I thought you liked Zsa Zsa's pussy?"

The flea says, "I did, but somehow I'm back in Al Hirt's beard." [294]

• • •

What is the world's greatest douche powder? Alum, LSD, and Ky. Colonel Fried Chicken. It's up tight, out of sight, and finger-lickin' good. [295]

• • •

Why is graduating from UCLA like eating pussy? Even though you do it, you don't brag about it. [297]

• • •

Guy goes to Las Vegas and gives a bellhop $100 for a girl with great big tits and a small pussy. This gorgeous blonde shows up at the door and says, "Are you the guy with the big mouth and the small cock?" [298]

• • •

A man goes to a druggist and asks if he has any Sex-Lax. The druggist says, "Do you mean Ex-Lax?"

The man says, "No, I mean Sex-Lax. I don't have any trouble going." [311]

• • •

Two guys and a girl were washed up on a tropical island. After the first week, the girl was so embarrassed at what she was doing that she killed herself.

RUDE & CRUDE

The guys kept screwing her, but after the second week, the guys were so embarrassed at what they were doing that they buried her.

After the third week, they were so embarrassed at what they were doing, that they dug her up. [336]

• • •

Man at a urinal looks down at his cock and says, "Today is my 60th birthday. It's too bad you didn't live to see it." [341]

• • •

After a drunken orgy a man wakes up in his bedroom, but sees only a bra, panties, and shoes. He groans and says, "You don't suppose I ate the whole thing, do you?" [342]

• • •

A castaway jacked off so much he couldn't get a hard-on. So he looks out at the horizon and says, "There's a ship!" He says, "There's a beautiful woman rowing to shore!" He says, "She's nude and walking toward me!" His cock gets hard. He grabs his cock and says, "Now I've got you, you little bastard, and moreover, I lied. There was no ship out there." [348]

• • •

A man is viewing the Grand Canyon. He falls and to save himself he grabs a woman's tits. She indignantly says, "Sir please move your hands." [The man moves his fingers in and out.] [352]

• • •

After six martinis, a man turns to this beautiful girl next to him and says, "How about having a good fuck at my place?" She hits him with her purse.

He says, "OK. How about a good fuck at your place?" She hits him harder with her purse.

RUDE & CRUDE

The man says, "I suppose considering the foul mood you're in, a blow job is out of the question." [353]

• • •

Hear about the guy who was arrested for masturbating on an airplane? It was for skyjacking. [359]

• • •

Definition of a fierce competitor: Someone who comes in first and third in a masturbation contest. [365]

• • •

Know the zip code for sex? Well if you did, you'd get more. [366]

• • •

Sierra Club motto: Eat a beaver and save a tree. [368]

• • •

The sex act is a misdemeanor in California. The more you miss, the meaner you get. [369]

• • •

A Texan wants to become a member of a Bedouin tribe. The chief says, "Well you have to pass three tests. First, drink a quart of this secret tribal liquor. Second, pull an ulcerated tooth from my pet tiger. Third make love to a frigid Bedouin girl. Each is in one of the three tents in front of you."

The Texan goes into the first tent and drinks the quart of liquor. He goes into the second tent and there is much screaming and roaring. He comes out still drunk from the secret tribal liquor and says, "OK, where is that broad with the bad tooth?" [370]

• • •

Two snails are making love. After they're through, a caterpillar says to one of them, "You certainly know how to eat escargot." [371]

RUDE & CRUDE

• • •

A man goes into a restaurant and the waitress is a snotty bitch. So he says, "I want a BLT C-U-N-T."

The waitress says, "You can't talk to me that way."

The man says, "I just wanted a BLT, Cut Up Not Toasted."

The waitress comes back with a very soggy BLT sandwich and says, "Here's your BLT S-H-I-T."

The man asks, "What does that mean?"

The waitress says, "BLT Should've Had It Toasted."

The man says, "F-U-C-K Y-O-U."

The waitress says, "What does that mean?"

The man says, "FUCK YOU." [405]

• • •

A Polish girl goes to Western Union, but finds it is closed. She knocks on the window and the clerk says, "Sorry we're closed."

The girl says, "But I've got to send a message to my mother on Mother's Day and I'll do anything."

The clerk looks at her big tits and says, "Anything?" The girl says yes so the clerk takes the girl into the back room and he says, "OK, get down on your knees." The girl does and the clerk says, "OK, pull down my zipper and take out my cock." She does. The clerk says, "Now take hold of it and go ahead."

The Polish girl grabs his cock and says to the end of it, "Hello, Mother?" [407]

• • •

RUDE & CRUDE

A guy is complaining about his dumb girlfriend who came back from the doctor's office and said she can't remember if the doctor told her she had VD or TB. His friend says, "Well what are you going to do on your date tonight?"

The guy says, "Well if she coughs, I'll fuck her." [409]

• • •

One male sperm practices to be first into the vagina. He practices and practices swimming. He hears the bell and leads the pack downstream. Suddenly he stops and starts to swim upstream. Another sperm asks why.

He says, "It's a hand job." [433]

• • •

A guy bought an inflatable woman through the mail. He blew her up but then wrote a letter to the manufacturer asking for his money back. When asked what went wrong, the man said, "Well, I bit her on the neck she farted and flew out the window." [464]

• • •

Know why women have legs? So they won't leave snail trials on the sidewalk. [497]

• • •

Know the NASA definition of a woman? A life-support system for a pussy. [498]

• • •

You know when I was young, my cock was so stiff I couldn't bend it with my hands. You know it's amazing how strong my hands have gotten in the last 40 years. [503]

• • •

A woman owns a cat that continually gets sick from hairballs. She goes to the druggist and says, "I want to remove all the hair from my little pussy." The druggist brings her a depilatory and the woman says, "Should I take any precautions with this medicine?"

The druggist says, "Don't ride a bicycle for a week." [513]

• • •

Know what you get when you cross a rooster with an owl? A cock that's up all night. [515]

• • •

Know what total rejection is? When you're jacking off, your hand falls asleep. [561]

• • •

Polish wedding announcement? U-,- wedding--Stella-Mr.--. [562]

• • •

God didn't make Eve from Adam's rib, but from his anus. That's why women have been a pain in the ass ever since. [569]

• • •

A man who had 5 cocks was asked how his shorts fit. The man said, "Like a glove." [582]

• • •

Know the definition of a perfect woman? She's 3 feet tall, has big tight lips, and has a flat spot on top of her head where you can set your drink. [596]

• • •

Know why the Star Trek Starship Enterprise is like a piece of toilet paper? Because they both circle Uranus looking for Klingons. [617]

• • •

Know the difference between a genealogist and a gynecologist? A genealogist looks up the family tree and the gynecologist looks up the family bush. [631]

• • •

Difference between a pig and a sailor? A pig won't spend all night trying to fuck a sailor. [632]

• • •

A man goes into a cafe and says, "Give me some ham and eggs."

The waitress says, "What you want is scratched."

The man says, "I know, but wash your hands and bring me some ham and eggs." [633]

• • •

Know the difference between a woman and a toilet seat? When you are finished, the toilet seat doesn't follow you around. [658]

• • •

When God was resting on the 7th day, an angel told him that he had some parts left over. He looked down and said, "Put the cunts on the dumb ones." [660]

• • •

A guy goes into a bar and orders two very dry martinis. He drinks one and pours the other on his right hand. The bartender says, "Why did you do that?"

The guy whispered, "I'm trying to get my date drunk." [664]

• • •

Know how to eat a frog? Put one leg behind each of your ears. [665]

RU DE & CRUDE

• • •

Know how many animals are in the average pair of pantyhose? One ass, one pussy, calves, 10 little piggies, 20 crabs and a dead fish no one can find. [689]

• • •

Guy meets a girl in a bar and after a while she gets excited and agrees to take him to her apartment. She says, "Follow me to my apartment; I've got an itchy pussy."

The guy says, "You better point it out to me. I can't tell one Japanese car from another." [735]

• • •

Know the difference between a pussy and a cunt? A pussy is that nice soft wet thing you like to play with. A cunt is the bitch that owns it. [749]

• • •

Tarzan asks Jane, "What-your name?"

Jane says, "Jane."

Tarzan says, "What whole name?"

Jane says, "Cunt." [750]

• • •

Guy says to a waitress, "Anheuser-Busch."

The waitress says, "Fine, and how's your cock?" [752]

• • •

Hear they have found a use for used tampon? Tea bags for vampires. [770]

• • •

RUDE & CRUDE

Know why a tampon has a string on it? So you can floss after eating. [774]

• • •

A guy doesn't know if his girlfriend has AIDS or Alzheimer's and asked his friend what to do. His friend says, "Drop her off a mile from home and if she finds her way back don't fuck her." [776]

• • •

What is a slut? A woman who will sleep with anyone.

What is a bitch? A woman who will sleep with anyone but you. [793]

• • •

A woman sees a 12" -inch condom with 1" -inch ribs sticking out on all sides. She asks the country store owner what it was used for. The owner says, "Well I'm not sure, but I know it will lift a sheep 3' off the ground." [794]

• • •

Veteran who had his balls shot off in Vietnam was interviewing for a job with the post office. When the interviewer found out about his injury he said, "The job is yours." The Vet said, "What is the salary and hours?" The interviewer said, "Well you start at $1200 a month and the normal hours are 8 to 4, but you can come in at 9." The Vet says, "I don't want any special treatment." The interviewer said, "Well you can come in at 9 because when we get to work we normally just stand around for an hour scratching our balls." [804]

• • •

A midlevel employee got a phone call telling him to see the company doctor and leave urine, stool and semen samples. A high level executive got a similar message and his executive secretary returns the doctor's office call and says, "Is it okay if I send over a pair of his shorts via company mail?" [805]

RU|DE & CRUDE

• • •

Hear about the new female robot? It is the improved model and has just 3 settings: Fuck, suck, and off. [809]

• • •

If a stork brings white babies and a crow brings black babies, what brings no babies? A swallow. [818]

• • •

Know how to offend a Jewish American Princess? Butt fuck her and wipe your dick on her drapes. [820]

• • •

A very pretty woman goes to a young gynecologist. The woman finds it painful and jumps up when he tries to examine her vaginally. The gynecologist says, "I won't be able to examine you if I don't numb your vagina. Is that ok?"

When she says yes, the gynecologist puts his head between her legs and goes, "Numb, numb, numb." [840]

• • •

Know what a bucking bronco fuck is? You mount your wife from the rear; , grab her by the hair, and whisper into her ear:, "This is the way your sister likes it." [842]

• • •

A white-collar criminal was put in prison with a 250-pound 6-foot Black Panther. The first time they were alone, the black said, "We are going to live in this cell like we were married." The white groaned. The black said, "Don't worry. I'm going to be the wife." The white sighed with relief. The black then said, "Now come over here and suck your wife's cock." [855]

• • •

A man lost his cock in the war and they grafted on an elephant trunk. It worked fine most of the time, but at a formal dinner party he was sitting next to a pretty girl. His cock got out of his pants, grabbed a dinner roll, and disappeared.

The girl said, "Gee, I'd like to see you do that again."

The guy says, "I don't think my asshole can take another dinner roll right now." [862]

• • •

Three guys are talking about what animal they would like to be. One says, "A gorilla because they are so powerful."

The second guy says, "A panther because they are so fast."

The third says, "A whale." When asked why he says, "Because they have a 6-foot tongue and an air hole to breathe through." [868]

• • •

Young son comes home from school and asks, "Dad what's a cunt?"

Dad says, "Where did you hear that word?"

The kid says, "At school."

Father takes his son into the library and opens a big medical dictionary showing a picture of a female body. The father points between the female's legs and says, "Son that's a vagina. Everything around it is a cunt." [889]

• • •

A man and a woman meet in a bar and get the hots for each other. When they get to her apartment, she rips her clothes off and says, "Make me feel like a woman."

The guy rips his clothes off, throws them in a corner, and says, "Iron those." [911]

RUDE & CRUDE

• • •

Man takes his new girlfriend to a mountain cabin in winter. She asks him to go outside and get some wood for the fireplace. He says, "I don't have any gloves and my hands will freeze."

She says, "If you get some wood, I'll let you warm your hands by putting them between my legs." So he goes outside and brings in some wood and lights a fire. He puts his hands between her legs and gives her a big kiss. They continue to kiss but the fire goes out. So the same thing happens. He comes in with the wood and starts to move his hands around and gives her a big kiss. The fire goes out a third time, so he goes out and gets some more wood.

When he comes over to sit next to his girlfriend, she has gotten very aroused and says, "Don't your ears ever get cold?" [919]

• • •

Know why women are unique? They can bleed for a week and not die; they can give milk without eating grass; they can bury a bone and not get dirt on their nose. [921]

• • •

What do two lesbians do when they are both menstruating? They fingerpaint. [929]

• • •

An old man and old woman meet at a nursing home. They hit it off and after a while they would sit on her couch every evening in her room. She would put a blanket over their laps and she would play with his private parts while they watched TV.

After a couple of months, he didn't show up at the appointed time. She went looking for him and found him in another woman's room sitting on the couch with a blanket over their laps watching TV.

She said, "What has this woman got that I don't have?"

He said, "Parkinson's." [933]

• • •

Know the difference between a woman and a computer? A woman won't take a 3½-inch floppy. [942]

• • •

Pick up lines:

You have great legs, when do they open?

You have 206 bones in your body. Want to try for 207?

Do you sleep on your stomach? No, -i-? Is it OK if I do?

That's a pretty dress, but it would look better lying on my bedroom floor. [946]

• • •

A scientist perfected a bra that totally masked a woman's nipples and prevented her breasts from bouncing as she walked. Fortunately, his fellow scientists took him out in the parking lot and beat the shit out of him and the product never got on the market. [964]

• • •

A school had a lot of trouble with some students saying, "N****rs suck, spics suck, fags suck," so they banned the word suck.

A little 7 year old girl came up to a teacher after playground was over and said, "Johnnie said a bad word."

The teacher said, "What was the word?"

The girl said, "I can't say it."

The teacher said, "You have to tell me or I can't discipline Johnnie."

The little girl said, "Well, I can't say the word, but I will say it rhymes with 'fuck.'" [965]

• • •

Know the generic term for Viagra? Mycocksafloppin. [968]

• • •

Why are women like dog turds? The older they are, the easier they are to pick up. [971]

• • •

A man in a bar asks the pretty woman next to him if he can buy her a drink. She says, "No. Alcohol is bad for my legs."

The man says, "It causes them to swell?"

The woman says, "No, it causes them to spread." [979]

• • •

A grandfather takes his grandson to Disneyland. It is a crowded weekend and they become separated. The kid goes up to a guard and says, "I've lost my grandfather."

The guard, trying to help identify the grandfather in the crowds, says, "What does your grandfather like?"

The kid thinks a minute and says, "Jack Daniels and girls with big tits." [981]

• • •

At a Madison Square Garden boxing event, the announcer says, "And now Susan Schwartz will sing the National Anthem."

A drunk yells out and says, "Susan Schwartz is a fat, ugly cocksucker."

RUDE & CRUDE

The announcer says, "Nevertheless, Susan Schwartz will now sing the National Anthem." [992]

• • •

A little girl, Susan, gets home late from school and her mother says, "Where have you been?"

The girl says, "I was doing cartwheels for the boys."

The mother says, "Susan, the little boys just want to see your panties."

Susan says, "I know mother. That's why I take my panties off before I do the cartwheels." [993]

• • •

A woman gets on an elevator and the man on the elevator says, "Can I smell your pussy?"

The woman says, "Of course not, you pervert."

The man says, "Then it must be your feet." [994]

• • •

Biker T-shirts:

"Tell your breasts to stop staring at my eyes."

"If you can read this, it means the bitch fell off." [1003]

CHAPTER 16
SEX

Sweet and sticky— It's our favorite subject, and well fleshed out here.

~-~-~~-~-~~-~-~

Drunk says, "Honey, aren't you sort of dry?"

His girlfriend looks down and says, "Move up, stupid, -. You're licking the rug." [54]

• • •

Did you hear about the girl who was so shy, that she would only let her boyfriend eat her when she sat on his eyes? [72]

• • •

Know when a cub scout becomes a boy scout? When he eats his first brownie. [73]

• • •

Know what a 68 is? That's where your girlfriend owes you one. [75]

• • •

Know what an anchovy is? It's a fish that smells like a finger. [77]

• • •

Know what a drip-dry prick is? It's a prick too short to shake. [78]

• • •

A woman is sitting in a theater, and whispers to her husband, "The man next to me is masturbating."

SE|X

The husband says, "Just ignore him."

The wife says, "I can't, he's using my hand." [80]

• • •

What's pink and pretty and can fuck all night? (Stick out tongue.) [112]

• • •

Arnold Palmer staggers into Tom Watson's room after screwing a local nympho 5 times in an hour and says, "Christ what's par on that hole?" [113]

• • •

Cinderella was told by the fairy godmother that if she didn't get back by midnight her pussy would be changed into a pumpkin. Cinderella didn't show up until 3 in the morning.

(Walk bowlegged.) The fairy godmother said, "I told you what would happen."

Cinderella said, "Yeah but you didn't tell me I would meet a guy named Peter, Peter." [115]

• • •

A guy sees a girl in very tight stretch pants. He says, "How do you get into those?"

The girl looks him over and says, "Well, let's start with a coupla very dry martinis." [120]

• • •

A 70-year-old man remarries and on his wedding night, he spreads his fingers apart and shows his hand to his new bride. She says, "Does that mean we're going to do it 5 times?"

The groom says, "No. Pick a finger." [137]

• • •

A nun and a priest are making their weekly visit on a camel to a remote Sahara village when half way from nowhere, the camel dies. After 2 days with no water, the priest says to the nun, "I'm afraid we're going to die, and I've never seen a naked woman."

The nun said, "I've never seen a naked man."

So they both take all their clothes off.

The nun points to the priests private parts and said, "What is that?"

The priest is embarrassed and finally says, "Well, it's the source of all life."

The nun says, "Well, for Christ's sake, stick it in the camel and let's get the hell out of here." [149]

• • •

A priest is playing golf with a nun for his caddie. The priest slices his first shot into a lake and says, "Oh shit."

The nun says, "God will punish you for swearing."

The priest keeps swearing and after a particularly long string of cusswords, the clouds part, there is a thunder clap and a bolt of lightning flashes down, but slices to the left and hits the nun.

A deep voice from the heavens says, "Oh shit." [150]

• • •

A girl goes to her doctor for a complete physical. The doctor notices that there is wax in her belly button and asks her about it. The girl says, "Don't worry, it's just that my boyfriend likes to eat by candlelight." [151]

• • •

A girl told her friend that she went to Vegas with her boyfriend. The girlfriend said, "Aren't you afraid of the Mann act?"

The girl said, "No. As a matter of fact, I kinda enjoy it." [169]

• • •

The boss calls a junior member of the firm to come into his office and closes the door. He says, "Are you screwing my secretary?"

The junior says, "Oh, no sir."

The boss says, "Good. *You* fire her." [170]

• • •

Definition of a nymphomaniac: A woman who will make love to a man within 15 minutes after she has her hair done. [191]

• • •

What's better than honor? Inner. [192]

• • •

Pierre the Cajun came home from work and sat down for dinner. He asked his wife where #1 son was. His wife said, "He was eaten by the alligators."

The Cajun goes to bed and fucks his wife. The next day he comes home from work and sits down for dinner. He asks where his #2 son is. His wife says, "He was eaten by the alligators."

Pierre goes to bed and fucks his wife. The next day he comes home from work and sits down to dinner. He asks where #3 son is. His wife says, "He was eaten by the alligators."

SE|X

He slams his fist down on the table and says, "Woman, you think I work all day and fuck all night just to feed the alligators?" [216]

• • •

King Arthur is going to the First Crusade, but is worried about his wife being faithful to him. He goes to the royal armorer and asks him to make the best chastity belt money can buy. Two weeks later, the King returns and the royal armorer shows him a beautifully made chastity belt but it had a hole where it shouldn't.

When the King says, "What good will this do?" the Armorer puts a carrot in the hole and a hidden blade slices it off. The King is happy and goes off on the Crusade. After he returns, he assembles all the Knights and nobles who stayed home to protect the Kingdom and orders a short arm inspection. He finds that each of their cocks have been cut off except Sir Lancelot.

He says to Sir Lancelot, "I want to thank you for your loyalty."

[Put tongue on back of lower front teeth.] Lancelot says, "You're welcome, Your Majesty." [218]

• • •

A man with a very small cock finally talked his girl into letting him just put the head in. He naturally stuck it all in. The girl got excited and said, "Give me all of it."

The guy says, "No, a deal's a deal." [225]

• • •

Mixed emotions: When you see your teenage daughter come in after a date at 2 a.m. with a Gideon bible under her arm. [238]

• • •

SEX

Mother comes home and tells her husband, "Do you know our son is studying psychology where they study things like sex perversion and masturbation?"

The father goes up to the son's room and sees him masturbating. The father says, "When you're done with your homework, I want to talk to you." [300]

• • •

Manager of a swinging singles apartment is trying to rent an apartment to a prospective tenant. He says, "On Fridays, the girls throw their keys into the pool and you get to sleep with the girl if you bring up her keys."

The tenant says, "That's too impersonal."

The manager says, "Well, on Saturdays everyone brings a bottle of vodka and we have a drunken orgy in the sauna."

The tenant says, "I don't drink."

The manager says, "You're not gay, are you?" The tenant says no. The manager says, "Well, you won't like Sundays either." [326]

• • •

Know how Linda Lovelace plays with herself? (Clear throat) [372]

• • •

Secretary tells her boss that she has good news and bad news. The boss says, "What's the good news?"

The secretary says, "You're not sterile." [377]

• • •

Did you ever go to bed with an ugly woman? No, but I woke up with a few. [379]

• • •

Hear Linda Lovelace's talent was hereditary? Yes, her mother went down on the *Titanic*. [381]

• • •

Adam starts to make love to Eve for the first time and Eve backs up a few paces. Adam says, "What's wrong?"

Eve says, "I'm backing up as I don't know how big this thing is going to get." [404]

• • •

Know why God made crotch hair curly? So it wouldn't poke you in the eye. [414]

• • •

Definition of a tiger? A 500-pound pussy that eats you. [452]

• • •

Know why Helen Keller masturbated with her left hand? Because she moans better with her right hand. [454]

• • •

A couple went to a marriage counselor and on their first visit the counselor said, "Do you have mutual orgasms?"

The woman said, "No, we are with Mutual of Omaha." [458]

• • •

The only thing bad about eating pussy is the view. [465]

• • •

Definition of a penis? A one-eyed snake in a turtleneck sweater. [466]

• • •

Know the difference between beating your fish and beating your meat? If you beat your fish it will die. [467]

• • •

Hear about the sex life of an egg? It gets laid once and eaten once. [468]

• • •

How to find a fat woman's pussy? Roll her in flour and look for the wet spot. [474]

• • •

Know what you get when combine a 5# pound cat with a 5-pound jar of peanut butter? You get a 10-pound pussy that sticks to the roof of your mouth. [479]

• • •

One girl is complaining about her boyfriend's dandruff. Her girlfriend says, "Give him Head and Shoulders."

The girl says, "How do you give your boyfriend shoulders?" [486]

• • •

If only Josephine had known about fellatio. She could have blown Napoleon's Bonaparte. [487]

• • •

Husband asks his wife, "How come you never tell me when you have an orgasm anymore?"

The wife says, "You're never there." [505]

• • •

What's better than roses on your piano? Tulips on your organ. [507]

• • •

What do you call a call girl who can suck a golf ball through a garden hose? "Darling." [509]

• • •

Know what you call a nurse with dirty knees? The head nurse. [519]

• • •

Do you know that 2/3 of all woman play with themselves at least once a week? Do you know what the other 1/3 does? (Wait for answer "No") It figures. [522]

• • •

As the flasher said, "I think I'll stick it out one more year." [524]

• • •

Know the difference between a drum and a blow job? You can't beat a blow job. [528]

• • •

As the hurricane said to the palm tree, "Hold on to your nuts . This is going to be a wild and crazy blow job." [546]

• • •

A man and a snow storm are a lot alike. You never know how deep they are going to be or when they are coming. [547]

• • •

St. Peter was complaining to God about the low moral standards prevalent in the world. God thought a minute and said, "What we can do is send a plaque to all those people who don't engage in oral sex." [To your audience) "Do you know what the plaque said? No? Well I didn't get a plaque either." [552]

• • •

Eating pussy is a dark and thankless job, but somebody has got to do it. [592]

• • •

SEX

What's long and black and full of seamen? A submarine. [609]

• • •

A husband comes home drunk and horny. His wife is asleep with her mouth open. The husband puts two aspirin in her mouth. The wife chokes and says, "Why did you put aspirin in my mouth? I don't have a headache."

The husband says, "Good. Let's have sex." [626]

• • •

Know the three most dangerous flight risks? Two flight instructors in a single plane and a stewardess with a broken tooth. [630]

• • •

Boy deaf mute tells a girl deaf mute, "If you want to make love, pull my penis once. If you don't want to make love, pull my penis 20 times." [677]

• • •

Man goes to a doctor. Doctor says, "I've got good news and bad news. The bad news is that you have 6 months to live." Man asks what the good news is. The doctor says, "You remember my receptionist, the blonde with the big tits? I'm fucking her." [681]

• • •

A neighbor got a new hunting rifle. He went next door to his neighbor and offered him a chance to go hunting with it in the hills above their houses. They got to the top of the hill and the gun owner stopped to rest and aimed his gun with its powerful telescopic sight on his neighbor's house. He said, "I can see your wife in your bedroom. She's totally naked and there's a nude man next to her."

The neighbor says, "That bitch said she was going shopping. Shoot her in the head and shoot his cock off."

SE|X

The gun owner looks again in the telescopic sight and said, "I think I can get them both with one shot." [684]

• • •

A wife is not happy with her infrequent sex life and so tries to arouse her husband by buying and wearing crotchless panties she got at Victoria's Secret. The husband comes home from work sits down with the paper and a drink. The wife nosily sits in front on him and spreads her legs. The husband finally looks at her and says, "Are you sitting on the cat?" [703]

• • •

The Boss was trying to encourage a despondent employee and tells him that when he gets depressed, he goes home and screws his wife for lunch and he feels much better in the afternoon. The next day the boss sees the employee, who is smiling. The boss says, "Did you take my advice?"

The employee says, "I sure did and Boss, you sure have a beautiful house." [730]

• • •

Hear about the blind skunk who tried to fuck a fart? [734]

• • •

How do you tell a good blow job? When you can't get out of bed because the sheets are stuck in your asshole. [738]

• • •

Presidents Reagan, Obama, and Clinton were on a boat that hit an iceberg. Reagan said, "Save the women and children."

Obama said, "Fuck the women and children."

Clinton said, "Do we have time?" [746]

• • •

SE X

Husband comes home and his wife says, "What did the doctor say?"

The husband says, "The doctor tells me I've only got 24 hours to live."

The wife says, "What do you want to do?"

The husband says, "How about making love?"

The wife says, "No., from what you said I've got to get up early for a funeral tomorrow." [763]

• • •

A nun gets on a game show. The first question is, "Who was the first man?" The nun says, "Adam." Bells and lights go off.

The second question is, "Who was the first woman?" The nun says, "Eve." Bells and lights go off.

The third question is, "What was the first thing Eve said?" The nun says, "That's a hard one." Bells and lights go off. [764]

• • •

What do you get if you cross a hooker with a pit bull? Your last blow job. [786]

• • •

Guy goes into a bar and says, "I want three shots of your strongest whiskey."

Bartender says, "Celebrating something?"

Guy says, "Well I just had my first blow job."

Bartender says, "Good enough if you want a 4th it's on the house."

SE|X

The guy says, "OK, if the first three don't get the taste out of my mouth." [803]

• • •

Woman goes to a veterinarian complaining that every time she bends over, her big Doberman screws her doggie style. The vet says, "Why don't you have him castrated?"

The woman says, "Can't you just clip his nails?" [808]

• • •

Know why gerbils can't drive? They're always stuck in Geere. [845]

• • •

Hear about Geere and the Disney studios? The good news is that Geere is going to make a movie for Disney. The bad news is that Mickey Mouse is missing. [847]

• • •

Two cops are walking through the morgue and they see a black corpse with a 12-inch dick. One cop says, "I've got a dick just like that."

The other cop says, "You mean 12 inch long?"

The first cop says, "No, dead." [849]

• • •

Know the hardest thing about eating a bald pussy? Getting the diaper back on. [865]

• • •

An Irishman comes over from Ireland to England and spends his first paycheck getting drunk in a pub. He wakes up with a terrible hangover and a policeman is taking him to jail. He comes up before the judge and the judge says, "Paddy, you are charged with necrophilia."

Paddy says, "What's necrophilia?"

The judge says, "It is having sex with a dead person."

Paddy says, "I'm sorry, your honor, I just thought she was English." [879]

• • •

Mike Tyson grabs a girl and screws her. When it's over he asks her, "How was it?"

She says, "Do you want the good news or the bad news?"

Tyson says, "The good news."

She says, "You're two inches longer than Magic Johnson." [896]

• • •

What is the difference between a microwave and butt fucking? A microwave doesn't brown your meat. [932]

• • •

Know what Social Security sex is? A little every month, but not enough to live on. [958]

• • •

Little girl said, "I saw that Daddy's peepee was in your peepee."

Mother said, "That's the way you get a baby."

The little girl said, "I also saw Daddy's peepee in your mouth."

The mother said, "That's the way you get jewelry." [960]

• • •

One woman says to another, "You've been out with Ed. He's asked me out. What can I expect?"

The other woman says, "Well, he will pick you up in a limo. He will take you to a wonderful little restaurant where you will have a marvelous meal and delicious wine. Then he will take you to a very romantic little club where you can dance and listen to the palm trees in the wind and the waves on the ocean. But then after he takes you home, he'll rip your dress off and ravish you repeatedly."

The woman says, "But what is your advice?"

The other woman thinks and says, "Wear an old dress." [978]

• • •

Why do brides smile when they are walking down the aisle? They know they won't have to give any more blow jobs. [982]

• • •

A nine year old girl asks her mother, "Why is Daddy divorcing you?"

She says, "That's none of your business."
The girl says, "How much do you weigh?"

The mother says, "That's also none of your business."

The little girl says, "How old are you?"

The mother says, "That's also none of your business. Stop asking such questions."

The little girl tells her best friend what happened.

Her friend says, "When your mother isn't looking, look at her driver's license. It will answer all of your questions."

SE X

The little girl gets the mother's driver's license out of her purse and looks at it. That night the little girl says, "Mommy I know how old you are."

The mother says, "How old am I?"

The girl says, "37."

The mother says, "That's right, how did you know that?"

The little girl says, "I also know how much you weigh."

The mother says, "How much?" The little girl says, "137 pounds."

The mother says, "That's right. How do you know all these things?"

The little girl says, "I also know why daddy is divorcing you."

The mother says, "Why?"

The little girl says, "You got an 'F' in sex." [998]

• • •

An attractive Jewish woman was widowed in her late 30s and after a year of mourning on a weekend put on a bikini and went to a secluded beach to sunbathe. After a month of sun bathing, a handsome young Jewish man put his blanket next to hers and started to sunbathe. The woman was attracted to him and said, "I haven't seen you here before."

The man said well, "My wife died about a year ago and after a year in mourning I decided to go to the beach."

Now the woman was really attracted to him. Not wanting the conversation to die, and being a cat lover, she said: "Do you like pussy cats?"

SEX

With that he jumped up, ripped off her bikini and made wild passionate love to her. It was the best sex she had ever had. She said, "How did you know I wanted you to do that?"

The man said, "How did you know my name was Katz?" [999]

• • •

Do you know what a woman's breasts have in common with toy trains? Even though they were both designed for children, men like to play with them. [1004]

• • •

Little boy is beating some pots and pans. Little girl says, "What are you doing?"

Little boy says, "I'm a drummer."

Little girl says, "If you're a drummer, eat my pussy."

Little boy says, "I'm not a real drummer." [1012]

• • •

Difference between a dog and a fox? Three martinis. [1014]

• • •

What do you get if you combine Monica Lewinsky and Ted Kaczynski? A dynamite blow job. [1044]

• • •

The warning on the Viagra bottle says, "Swallow quickly or you will get a stiff neck." [1047]

• • •

A man is complaining about the sexual language children use today. "What do you tell your children?"

The counselor says, "Tell them that Fellatio is a Roman general and that Cunnilingus is an Irish airline." [1048]

CHAPTER 17
TOTALLY NUTS

More whacked and cracked than an elderly porn star, we put insane jokes here for safekeeping.

~ - ~ - ~ - ~ - - ~ - ~~ - ~ - ~

A black infant trying to talk says, "M-M-Mother."

The father says proudly, "Only 11 months old and already knows half a word." [18]

• • •

Multiply the number of times you have intercourse each month by 2. Add 5. Multiply result by 50. Add (2762 in 2012, 2763 in 2013, etc). Subtract the year of your birth. The first digit(s) is the number of times a month you have intercourse a month and the last two digits are your age. [36]

• • •

An American talking to a Frenchman mentions his distaste for the book *Lolita*. The Frenchman says, "I'm not familiar with the book. What is it about?"

The American says, "It's about a grown man making love to a thirteen-year-old."

The Frenchman says, "A thirteen-year-old what?" [48]

• • •

Know that 90% of all women with breast cancer have husbands who smoke? [74]

• • •

TO|TALLY NUTS

Dentists know that husbands of women who use Crest vaginal jelly have 30% fewer cavities. [76]

• • •

To view this "too hot to handle" joke—subscribe to our website www.DadsJokeBook.com. [117]

• • •

Woman goes to a doctor complaining that every time she sneezes she has an orgasm. The doctor says, "What are you doing for it?"

The woman says, "Sniffing pepper." [210]

• • •

Inmate in an insane asylum looks up at a seagull and it craps in his eye. An attendant says, "I'll go get some toilet paper."

The inmate says, "Don't bother, by the time you get back that seagull will be miles from here." [325]

• • •

Know the definition of a missed opportunity? A car full of n****rs going over a cliff with an empty seat. [331]

• • •

The doctors finally found out the cause of sickle cell anemia. Licking food stamps. [415]

• • •

A guy in a bar is sitting next to a beautiful blonde and after 5 martinis he can't resist her any longer so he grabs her breast and kisses it. She doesn't stop him so he grabs her pussy and sticks a finger in.

The girl says, "Would you please stick another finger in?"

The guy says, "OK, but why?"

The girl says, "I want to whistle to the bartender to throw your ass out of here." [428]

• • •

Know how to make a dead baby float? Put two scoops of dead baby in a glass of root beer. [575]

• • •

Know how you give CPR to an AIDS victim? [Blow in the air and stomp with your foot.)] [655]

• • •

What do 5000 battered women have in common? They can't keep their mouths shut. [833]

• • •

Know why a bald man has holes in his pockets? So he can run his fingers through his hair. [916]

• • •

Man comes home from work and sees his girlfriend packing. He says, "What are you doing?"

She says, "I'm leaving you. People say you're a bad man."

Man says, "What do you mean?"

She says, "They say you're a pedophile."

He says, "Wait a minute, that's a pretty big word for a 10 year-old, isn't it?" [945]

• • •

Did you hear they have developed a new wine for the incontinent? It's called Pinot More. [966]

• • •

What did the shark say near Indonesia? "This airline food ain't bad!" [1016]

TO|TALLY NUTS

• • •

Why is it hard to be a pedophile? You have to go to bed so early. [1017]

• • •

An older woman has a baby. She takes the baby home and a friend comes to her house to see the baby. The mother says, "You'll have to wait until it cries." The friend says, "Why?" The mother says, "I forgot where I put it". [1026]

• • •

Did you hear that Fight Club closed down? They couldn't get a decent Dental Plan. [1042]

• • •

Man hears about Lili's chili and goes to the grill and asks for Lili's chili. The waiter says, "I'm sorry it is sold out."

The patron next to him says, "I've only eaten half of mine. You can have it."

The man thanks him and when he finishes, he throws the chili up.

The man next to him says " ... that's about as far as I got." [1051]

CHAPTER 18
WHORES

It's the third oldest profession after bodyguard and chef, and here we prove that if it's physical comedy, it's therapy comedy.

~ - ~ - ~ ~ - ~ - ~ ~ - ~ - ~

A weatherman won a trip to Hawaii. When he got to the hotel room he asked the bellboy to send up a prostitute. When she got to the room she asked if he would like the weatherman special. He said, "Ok." With that, the whore took off his and her clothes. She then slapped his face with her tits.

The guy said, "What was that?"

The whore said, "That's the tropical breezes wafting over the palm trees." She then put her ass in his face and farted.

He said, "What was that?"

She said, "It was the sound of a distant volcano." She then stood over him and peed on him.

He said, "What was that?"

She said, "That was the gentle tropical rain."

With that he got out of bed and started to put his clothes on. She said, "Where are you going?"

He said, "Who can fuck in weather like this?" [17]

• • •

A man goes to a whorehouse and pulls down his pants,

exhibiting a 1-inch prick to the madam.

The madam says, "Who are you going to satisfy with that?"

The man says, "ME." [19]

• • •

A lumberjack comes out of the woods after having gone six months without a bath. He doesn't have any money and finally talks a whore into giving him a blow job in exchange for his lunch card. He opens his long johns and the whore starts sucking. She stops and looks up, saying, "Are you sure this is a clean place to eat?" [38]

• • •

Hooker gets in a cab but finds out she has no money. When she gets to her destinations she pulls up her dress and says, "How about if I pay for it with this." ?"

The cabbie takes one look and says, "Gee, lady, haven't you got anything any smaller?" [83]

• • •

A man goes to a whorehouse with an 18-inch prick. The Madam says, "Well, it's too big for my girls to screw you, but for $20.00 they could give you a blowjob."

The man says, "Christ, I could do that myself for free." [94]

• • •

A drunk gets the directions to a whorehouse mixed up and barges into the house of a truck driver, and starts to screw his wife. The truck driver comes home and grabs a butcher knife and grabs the drunk's balls, and says, "Have you got anything to say before I cut your balls off?"

The drunk says, "Yes. You've got a lot to learn about running a whorehouse." [95]

• • •

What do you get when you cross an elephant with a prostitute? A 500-pound whore who will work for peanuts. [102]

• • •

Man joins what he thinks is a prostitute club, but it turns out to be a parachute club. When the man finds out, he says, "My God. I've signed up for 3 jumps a week." [126]

• • •

A man goes to a whorehouse and pulls out his ½-inch hard-on and asks the madam what she can do for him. She finally remembers an older whore with a glass eye. She asks the whore to take out her glass eye and let this guy fuck it. She agrees, the customer screws the socket, and is ecstatic about how good it felt. He tells the whore that was great and he'd be back. The whore says, "I'll keep an eye out for you." [147]

• • •

An Israeli goes to NYC to find the sister of an Israeli girlfriend. He finds she's working in a whorehouse. She is good looking and after much negotiation she agrees to have an all night sex orgy with him for $200.

The next morning she says, "Will I see you again?"

The Israeli says, "No, I'm going back to Israel."

The whore says, "I've got a sister in Israel."

The Israeli says, "Yes I know she asked me to give you the envelope with $200 in it." [200]

• • •

A quadriplegic came to the door of a whorehouse. The madam opens the door and looks down and says, "I don't think I can do anything for you."

The quadriplegic says, "I rang the doorbell, didn't I?" [267]

• • •

A midget walks into a whorehouse and tugs on the skirt of the madam. The madam says, "How can we help you?" The midget pulls out the prettiest 14-inch cock the madam had ever seen in her 25 years in the business.

The madam says, "Can I play with it?"

The midget says "Yes, but you can't suck it."

The madam says, "Why?"

The midget says, "I had to stop girls from doing that. I used to be 6' tall." [285]

• • •

Union leader asks the madam if this is a union whorehouse. The madam says, "Yes."

The union leader says, "I'd like that young blonde in the corner."

The madam says, "No you get the old broad next to her with all the seniority." [292]

• • •

Man asks a prostitute what makes her hot, "Kissing your ears?"

She says, "No."

Man says, "Kissing your breasts?"

She says no.

Man says, "What then?"

Girl says, "Getting fucked without getting paid." [330]

• • •

WHORES

A woodsman came down out of the mountains after the snows melted and went to the local whorehouse. He was asked to first take a bath. While he was in the bath a young girl asked if he wanted a manicure. The woodsman didn't know what a manicure was but said, "Why not?"

He was a little nervous so the girl explained what she was going to do. She said, "Now I'm going to push back your cuticle."

The woodsman said, "If you'd stop playing with my hands, it would go back by itself." [399]

• • •

Hear about the drunk who woke up with his nose in an old whore's slipper and was afraid to open his eyes? [485]

• • •

A girl in a massage parlor was asked why she did this for a living. She said that she owed a lot of money to a loan shark named Paul and that she was rubbing Peter to pay Paul. [511]

• • •

The drunken sailor said to the whore, "How am I doing?"

The whore said, "You're doing 3 knots."

The sailor said, "What do you mean?"

The whore said, "You're not up, you're not in, and you're not getting your money back." [882]

• • •

Two prostitutes meet for coffee in a cafe early Monday morning. One asks the other what she did over the weekend. The other says she went to the movies but had to keep moving her seat. The first says, "Were you molested?"

The other says, "Eventually." [895]

• • •

What do you call a whore with a runny nose? Full. [898]

• • •

A Jewish prostitute meets a classmate at their high school 10 year class reunion. After a while she asks what he does. He says he's an accountant. He says, "What do you do?"

She says, "Well, frankly, I'm a prostitute."

The guy says, "Well I always wanted to have sex with you, how much will it cost me?"

The prostitute says, "$100."

The guy says, "I can't afford $100, but I can pay you $50."

They argue for a long while. The Jewish prostitute finally says, "OK, $50, but I'm telling you I won't be making a penny on this deal." [953]

Keyword Index

Actor
- Agent — MA-302
- Cannon — PG-156
- Shakespeare — CL-207

Adam & Eve
- Erection — SE-404
- Headache — MA-397

Idi Amin
- Killing — RA-461

Adultery
- Deathbed — MA-944
- Definition — CL-2
- Golf balls — MA-743
- Hold drink -- XXX — MA-363
- Hunting trip — MA-691
- Lawyer — LA-172
- Maternity ward — CL-278
- Motorcycle — CL-653
- Party — MA-823
- Ten Commandments — CL-358
- Three words — MA-810

Agent
- Actor — PG-156,
- Harmonica — MA-302

Aids
- Alzheimer's — RU-14
- Blacks — RU-776
- CPR -- XXX — RA-748
- Cure — TO-655
- Dentist — GA-724
- Funeral — GA-662
- Girlfriend — GA-733
- Hearing — GA-728
- Magic — GA-888
- Marriage — DO-822
- Miracle -- XXX — GA-719
- Pit bull — CL-777
- Research — GA-732
- Romantic — CL-704
- Statue of Liberty — GA-745
- Vegetables -- XXX — GA-719

Alaska
- JAP — MA-723

Alcohol
- Mormon — RA-984

Alien
- Allah — RE-417

Alligator
- Italians — RA-863
- Texan -- XXX — AN-51

Allen, Woody
- Movie — CL-900

Alzheimer's
- Aids — RU-776

Anchovy
- Definition — SE-77
- Angel — CL-167

Anniversary
- 25th — MA-96

Anorexic
- Ethiopian — RA-741

Anus
- Eve — RU-569

Arabs
- PLO — CL-725

Sheep	RA-858	Drunk	BA-315,
Texan	RU-370		RU-353,
Arkansas		XXX	BA-872
Marriage	PG-903	Fucking martini	CL-134
OJ Simpson	CR-941	Gay	BA-25,
ASCAP			GA-251
Starlet	CL-185	Itchy pussy	RU-735
Asparagus		Legs	RU-979
Oral sex	CL-679	Lottery	MA-254
Aspirin		Masturbation	RU-664
Wife	SE-626	Parrot	RA-816
Astronaut		Pleasant surprise	CL-324
Birth	CL-21	Screw anyone	BA-961
Black	AN-181	Tight pants	SE-120
Atomic radiation		Time	RU-266
Chernobyl	CL-739	Whistle	TO-428
Aunts		Baseball	
Cousins	CL-628	Adultery	MA-952
Auto theft		Gay	GO-27
Brown Cadillac	RA-360	Elephant	AN-589
Avalanche		Basketball	
Definition	CL-290	Lincoln	RA-448
		Bay Bridge	
Baboon		Longest	GA-566
Loma Linda	CL-697	Bears	
Bald		Christians	AN-784
Pockets	TO-916	Trap	DO-88
Staples	CL-534	Behind	
Balls		Beautiful	CL-140
Jolly Green Giant	CL-85	Belly button	
Moth	AN-84	Wax	SE-151
Baptism		Best man	
Black	RE-23	Bride	MA-10
Bar		Beverly Hills	
Douche bag	BA-567	Jews II	RA-462

Boxcar	RA-779	Dice	RA-190
San Fernando Valley	CL-712	Doberman Pincher	RA-791
Bikini		Ethiopians	RA-741
Nun	RE-118	Fuzz	RA-248
Bingo		Genie	RA-303
Old ladies	CL-906	Grocery store	RA-659
Bitch		Hang glider -- XXX	RA-510
Definition	RU-793	Heart Transplant	RA-259
Blacks		In tree -- XXX	TO-117
Abortion -- XXX	RA-698	Integration	RA-42
Al Sharpton	RA-178	Irish	RA-604
Idi Amin	RA-461	Javelin	RA-180
Alligator -- XXX	AN-51	Jesse Jackson	RA-798
Armadillos	RA-610	Jewish	RE-159
Astronaut	AN-181	King Kong	BA-624
Atlanta killer	RA-581, RA-585	Ku Klux Knievel -- XXX	RA-413
		Law degree	RA-139
Baby Sit -- XXX	CL-619	Lincoln	RA-448,
Baby talk	TO-18		RA-841
Baptism	RE-23	Long and hard -- XXX	RA-645
Big Cock	RA-700	Marry Jew	RA-204
Bird dog	AN-473	Marry Mexican -- XXX	RA-557
Black Panther	RU-855	Mike Tyson	SE-896
Blind -- XXX	RA-548	Menstruation -- XXX	RA-831
Break dance	RA-692	Military	AN-121
Cocoon	RA-602	Missed opportunity	TO-331
Cadillac	RA-50	Mormon	RA-754
Chains	RA-22	Mother Superior	RA-595
Civil Rights Worker	RA-22	NAACP	RA-108
Cotton Pickers	RA-767	National Geographic	RA-702
Crabs	RA-90	O.J. Simpson	CR-938,
Crime	RA-866		CR-939,
Cunt -- XXX	RA-661		CR-940,
Dead body	RA-205		CR-941
Definition, n****r	RA-599		

Olympic gold medalist	RA-702,	Trash Truck	RA-416
	RA-795	Washing machine	RA-108
Ownership -- XXX	RA-551	Water skiing	RA-114
Pall Bearers	RA-612	Watermelon	RA-769
Parrot	RA-816	Watts Pinata	RA-613
Plano, Texas	RA-625	Welfare Check -- XXX	RA-189
Police report	RA-205	Wet Suit	RA-549
Pope	RA-261	White bridegroom	RA-284
Post Office -- XXX	RA-344	White groom	RA-284
Rape -- XXX	DO-11,	White horse	RA-605
	RA-434	White man with blacks	RA-727
Red Eyes	RA-913	Wilt Chamberlain	MA-299
Renege	RA-455	Yeast Infection	RA-741
Rich Pryor	RA-673	Blonde	
Rodney King	RA-915	Roses	CL-963
Roy Rogers	RA-605	Ventriloquist	CL-976
Sammy Davis Jr.	RA-46,	BMW	
	RA-211,	Rolls Royce	PO-887
	RA-603	Boston strangler	
Scholarship	RA-180	Husband	MA-217
School	RA-306,	Boxing	
XXX	RA-645	National Anthem	RU-992
Semen, Urine -- XXX	RA-558	Boy Scout	
Shoe store	RA-622	Cub scout	SE-73
Sickle cell anemia	TO-415	Brainwash	
Sleep on beach	RA-573	Girlfriend	CL-101
Small Business	RA-930	Breasts	
Space Program	AN-181	Bra	RU-964
Steam bath -- XXX	RA-846	Hear Joke	RU-271
Submarine	SE-609	Implants	DO-785
Smoking	TO-74	Martinis	CL-40
Test Tube Baby	RA-611	Pleasant surprise	CL-324
Tire Chains	RA-641	Horse	AN-128
Toy trains	MA-1005	Kay and Edith	PG-127
Train -- XXX	RA-545	Breathalyzer	

Polish	RA-482	Purchasing agent	RU-168
Broad jump		Quick thinking	CL-495
Oral sex	RU-64	Secretary	SE-170,
Brownie			RU-805
Boy scout	SE-73	Union	WH-292
Brown, Jerry	PO-456	VP of sex and music	CL-398
Bug		Whorehouse	WH-95
Windshield	CL-666		
Butcher		**Cab Driver**	
Long Island duck	RA-432	Polack	RA-436
Bull		Woman	WH-83
Costume party	AN-86	Cabbage Patch doll	CL-717
Sweat	AN-68	Cad	
Bum		Definition	MA-532
Jesus	RE-160	Cadillac	
Pope	RE-577	Black	RA-50
Business		Cajun	
Bids	RA-475	Alligators	SE-216
Black	RA-930	Cake	PG-127
Boss	CL-963	California	
Bonus	MA-881	Culture	PG-875
Bridge builder	GA-122	Camel	
Budget	AN-128	G.I.	MI-143
Communications	RE-449	Priest/Nun	SE-149
Consultant	AN-245,	Texan	AN-6
	CL-247	Camelot	
Customer Relations	PG-123	Crusades	SE-218
Deal's a deal	SE-225	Cannibals	RU-43
Drunk	WH-95	Captain Hook	
Friend	AN-289	Jock Itch	CL-716
Genie	PG-104	Castaway	RU-336
Leadership	SE-730	Catholic	
Merger	AN-93	Bikini	RE-118,
Perfect Bra	RU-964		RE-161
Pig	AN-647	Buy baseball bat	MA-952

Camel	SE-149	Old	RU-503
Christ returns	RE-410	Potato	RA-574
Confessional	DO-129,	Cartwheels	RU-993
	GO-471,	Condom	CL-761
	RE-683	Disneyland	RU-981
Gays	GA-119	First sex	CL-307
Golf	RE-874	Gideon Bible	SE-238
Polish Pope	RA-489	Parents sex	SE-960
Pope and lawyer in Heaven	RE-607	Questions	SE-998
		Report card	RA-283
Pope blowjob	RE-493	Sexual relations	MA-240
Pope driving	PO-886	Son-in-law	MA-231
Virgin Mary	RE-638	Speech code	RU-965
Catholic Priest		Teacher name	RE-430
Adultery	DO-157	Chinese Restaurant	RA-177
Alter boy	RE-975	Christian	
Parrot	RE-980	Bears	AN-784
Pimple	RE-957	Coal Miner	
Swimming lesson	RE-927	Polack	RA-328
Cats		Cock	
Consultant	AN-245	Black	RA-700
Hairball	RU-513	Cobra	CL-674
Schizophrenic -- XXX	CL-45	Deals a deal	SE-225
Cecile B. DeMille		Elephant trunk	RU-862
Movie	RA-145	Hardon/wall	RU-202
Chapped lips		Iraqi	RA-563
Horseshit	CL-60	Irish arthritis	RA-58
Cheese		Jewish	MA-37
Israel	RE-652	Medium, Rare	CL-708
Chef Boyardee		Midget	WH-285
Balls	CL-30	Morgue	SE-849
Children		Quadriplegic	WH-267
Baby brother	AN-262	Transplant	RA-700,
Black	RA-306		RU-862
Bragging	CL-304	Wrinkles	CL-705

Cocktail waitress		Doberman Pincher	
Like a Manhattan	CL-9	Black	RA-791
Cow		Doctor	
Give birth	PG-650	Abscess	PG-686
Condom		AIDS	DO-822
Children	CL-761	Alzheimer's	DO-926
Druggist	DO-974	Blurry vision	DO-327
Duck	AN-802	Bridal exam	RU-840
Farmer	MA-635	Diagnosis	DO-345
Foot long	RU-794	Disease, CRS	CL-807
Leisure World	CL-815	Dogs	AN-20
Polack	RA-766	Eternal Youth	DO-568
Computer		Facelift	DO-373
JAP	RA-706	Feel good, look bad	DO-345
Country Club women	CL-713	Female doctor	DO-343
Cousins		Flying crabs	DO-69
Source	CL-628	Gangrene	DO-173
CPR		God	DO-445
AIDS	TO-655	Good news/bad news	DO-469,
Crusades	SE-218,		DO-726
	RA-243	Gynecologist	CL-3,
Crime			RU-631,
Definition	DO-483		RU-840
Dead baby float	TO-575	Gypsy	DO-89
		Heart attack	DO-252
Deaf Mute		Hunter	DO-88
Sex	SE-677	Long life	MA-723
Dental Plan	TO-1042	Medfly	DO-620
Dentist		Medicare	DO-316
AIDS	GA-662	Orgasm	DO-152
Balls	DO-264	Painful sex	MA-47
Crest vaginal jelly	TO-76	Polish	RA-694
Good dentist	DO-990	Psychiatrist	AN-63,
Disneyland			MA-183,
Child	RU-981		PG-541,

237

Psychiatrist cont.	DO-861	Drunk	
Purple prick	MA-49	Bald headed	CL-534
Receptionist	SE-681	Ballgame	PG-731
Sneezing	TO-210	Breathalyzer	RA-482
Sore elbow	AN-142	Bridegroom	RA-284
Taking history	DO-339	Food	CL-406
Testicle replacement	CL-268	Rug	SE-54
Thermometer	DO-87	Slipper	WH-485
Urologist	RU-187	Stolen car	RU-275
Vaseline	DO-136	Superman	BA-554
Dog		Ugly woman	SE-379
Doberman	RA-791, SE-808	Duck	
		Condom	AN-802
Gays	GA-196	Dyslexia	
Hump leg	AN-837	MDA	PG-835

Ear

Hunting	AN-92, AN-244		
Mother-in-law	AN-873	Oral sex	MA-56
Nigger	RA-791	Echo	
PMS	AN-838	Oral sex	RU-131
Poker	AN-891	Egg	
Seeing eye	AN-936	Sex life	CL-105, SE-468
Vietnamese cookbook	RA-529		
Welfare	AN-258	Elbow	
Douche		Breast	MA-98
Bag	CL-101	Elephants	
Bar	BA-567	Afro	AN-109
Powder	RU-295	Barrroom	AN-41
Druggist		Baseball	AN-589
Daughter's boyfriend	DO-974	Diarrhea	AN-106
Hearse	PG-174	Fly	AN-66
Pussy	RU-257, RU-513	Four feet	AN-588
		Man breathing	AN-539
Sexlax	RU-311	Prick transplant	RU-862
Tranquilizer	CL-124	Prostitute	WH-102

Quicksand	AN-107	Food Stamps	
Raped by	CR-82	Sickle Cell Anemia	TO-415
Sex with	CL-443	Football	
Tampon	AN-572	Dog	PG-856
Vibrator	AN-640	Iraqi	RA-857
Environmental impact report		Foreplay	
		Italian	RA-614
Sliver	DO-437	Fly	
Empire state bldg	PG-165	Queer Spider	AN-35
		Flying Crabs	DO-69

Face-lift

		Food shortage	RA-843
Van Dyke	DO-373	Ford, President	
Farmer		Contraceptive	PO-418
Newlyweds	MA-635	Fresca	CL-279
Ventriloquist	AN-648	Freeways	
Fart		When Safe	RA-460
Blind Skunk	SE-734	French	
Elephant	AN-41	Hunting	RA-273
Honda	PG-686	Lolita	PG-48
Retirement Home	PG-685	Luau	RU-53
Fat Woman		Frogs	
Find pussy	SE-474	Eat	RU-665
Fight Club closed down	TO-1042	Stork	AN-781
Finishing Schools		Gatorade	RA-395
Texas girls	CL-197		
Fish		## Gays	
Anchovy	SE-77	AIDS cure	DO-724
Kowalski	RA-362	AIDS definition	GA-646
Smell	CL-667	Alligator	BA-852
Flasher	SE-524	Attack a woman	GA-789
Flea		Bar bet	BA-580
Oral Sex	RU-294	Bar fight	GA-492
Toilet Seat	CL-16	Bay bridge	GA-566
Flight risks		Black eye	CL-111
Biggest	SE-630	Breakfast cereal	GA-499

Broken tooth	RA-139	Lucky	GA-654
Catholic	GA-119	Margarine	GA-924
Chicken	CL-775	Microwave	SE-932
Circumcision	GA-26	Military recruit	GA-811
Condom	GA-832	Missing	RA-814
CPR	TO-655	Mouth to mouth resuscitation	GA-472
Dangerous	RA-139		
Dentist	GA-662	Mustache	GA-601
Disney	SE-847	Navy	GA-909
Dog	GA-196	Olympics	RA-796
Employer	BA-25	Oral Roberts	GA-578
First blow Job	SE-803	Organ grinder	GA-215
French	GA-122	Parade	GA-690
Gays switch	GA-65	Refrigerator	GA-819
Gerbils	SE-845	Religion	GA-676
Golf	GA-472	Restaurant	GA-902
Governor Brown	PO-456, GA-618	Rock Hudson	GA-540, GA-718,
Hemorrhoids	RA-67		GA-720,
Herpes	CL-704		GA-721,
Hot lunch	GA-32		GA-729,
Hot tub	GA-759		GA-740
Hunting	AN-878	Schwartz	GA-208
In bar	GA-251	Scottish sergeant	MI-146
Jewish	CL-163, GA-910	Seafood	CL-393
		Shorts	GA-812
Job applicant	BA-25	Soldier	MI-110
Lesbian	GA-570, GA-576, GA-584, GA-587, GA-644, GA-788, GA-790, RU-929	Spider	AN-35
		Sports	GO-27
		Stool	GA-912
		Swinging singles	SE-326
		Switch	GA-65
		Talking tree	GA-988
		Tomboy	GA-309
		Tongue	GA-560

Unknown gay	GA-470	Rabbi cont.	RA-874
Weight loss	RA-148	Suck golf ball	SE-509
Whorehouse	GA-208	Two good balls	GO-227
Genealogist		Whorehouse	GO-890
Gynecologist	RU-631	Wife	GO-977
Genie		Gonorrhea Mean Joe	DO-637
A head	PG-104	Good Buddy Definition	GA-429
Black	RA-303	Grammar	
Gentlemen		Texas girls	CL-197
Definition	CL-5	Grand Canyon	RU-352
Gideon bible		Greek Jackie O.	RA-280
Daughter	SE-238	Restaurant	RA-177
Girdle		Gynecologist Def.	CL-3
Man	MA-224		
Glass eye		**H**ardware store	
Whorehouse	WH-147	Tea set	CL-755
Golden Gate Bridge	CL-61	Harmonica	
Golden toilet		Agent	RU-14
Drunk	RU-241	Harry Truman	RA-463
Golf		Head and Shoulders	
Bum	MA-950	Girlfriend	SE-486
Cold day	GO-338	Hearse	
CPR	GA-472	Druggist	PG-174
Five iron	DO-951	Heart attack	
Funeral	GO-880	Sex	DO-252
Gimme	GO-220	Helen Keller Doll	CL-7
God	DO-150	Masturbation	SE-454
Good News-Bad News	RE-425	Hemophiliac	
Heaven	RE-425	Prick	CL-675
Jesus	GO-446	Hemorrhoids	
Lesson	GO-555	Absence	CL-760
Moses	GO-446	Removal	RA-211
Orgasm	GO-623	Tender love	RA-67
Par	SE-113	Herpes	
Rabbi	RE-425,	Romantic	CL-704

Hillbilly		Wine	TO-966
Census	CL-480	Indians	
Hitler		Cowboy	CL-288
WWII	MI-506	Equal opportunity	RA-384
Hobos		Insane Asylum	
Dance	PG-71	Inmate	MA-1005
Homework		Seagull	TO-325
Psychology	SE-300	Inflatable doll	
Honda		Defective	RU-464
Fart	PG-686	Iraqi	
Menstrual cycle	RU-201	Circumcision	RA-563
Honor		Irish	
Better than	SE-192	Arthritis	RA-58
Hospital		Coffee with cream	PG-657
Explosion	DO-91	Cross with black	RA-604
Priest	DO-175	Driving	RA-885
Hunting		Dry cleaning	RA-996
Bears	AN-878	Fight	RA-985
Dog	AN-92, AN-244	Frontal lobotomy	RA-490
		Guinness brewery	RA-337
Trip	MA-691	IQ	DO-263
Hurricane		IRA	CL-894
Palm tree	SE-546	Irish maid pregnant	RA-983
Hypnotism		Men's tailor shop	RA-987
Preacher	RE-133	Mormon	RA-984
		Necrophilia	SE-879
Implants		Painting	RA-937
Breasts	DO-785	Physical exam	DO-892
Toilet paper	MA-943	Wake	RA-277
Incest		Wedding/wake	RA-780
Definition	CL-269	Italians	
Woody Allen	CL-900	Adultery	RA-272
Incontinent		Alligators	RA-863
Nose hair	RU-187	Crusades	RA-243
Signs	CL-226	Deathbed	RA-184

Foreplay	RA-614	Orgasms	RA-824
High school graduate	MA-426	Porno	RA-737
Navy ships	RA-188	Prostitute	WH-953
Spaghetti	CL-30	Saks 5th Ave.	RA-322
Wedding	MA-427	Stop fucking	RA-526
Wife	MA-24	Titanic	RA-542
WWII	RA-459	Trust me	RA-508
		Vampire	RA-523

Japanese

		Wailing wall	RE-751
Bar	BA-828	Waterbed	RA-634
Cataracts	RA-239	Widow oral sex	MA-512
Girls	RA-1007	Jews	
History	RA-463	Abortion	RA-586
Queef	RA-1007	Black convert	RE-159
Rice	RA-629	Black daughter-in-law	RA-222,
Jesus			RA-204
Mother	RE-198	Business bid	RA-475
Prince of Jews	RE-199	Catholic school	RA-559
Puerto Rican	RA-234	Chastity belt	RA-103
Nails	RA-670	Check	AN-747
Jewish American		Child molester	RA-850
Princess		Child's allowance	RA-931
Blowjob	RA-643	Christ returns	RE-160
Computer	RA-706	Christian martyrs	RA-145
Credit cards	RA-600	Circumcision	RA-639
Definition	RA-671	Crucifixion	RA-639,
Disease	RA-722		RA-670
Dream house	RA-696	Daughter	RA-520
Golfing	RA-439	Death camp	CL-806
Husband	RA-714	Dog style sex	MA-682
J.A.P.	RA-500	Drowning	RA-948
Jell-O	RA-757	Elephant	RA-496
Mexican maid	MA-564	Ethics	RA-502
Offend	RU-820	Fire	RA-203
Old Country	CL-712	Foreplay	RA-527

Gay	CL-163, GA-910	Urinal	RE-155
		Victoria Station	RA-779
Gentile Country club	RA-799	Virgin bride	MA-37
Honeymoon	RA-44	Wailing Wall	RE-751
Irish mayor	RA-801	Whorehouse	WH-200, RA-319
Israeli Egyptian tanks	RA-230		
Israeli wars short	RA-235	Widow oral sex	RA-453, MA-512
Jap Jew restaurant	RA-701		
Jewish fly	BA-949	Widow, bikini	SE-999
Jews II	RA-462	Jock itch	
Lifeguard	RA-948	Capt. Hook	CL-716
Loan	RA-948	Jolly Green Giant	CL-85
Long Island duck	RA-432		
Lottery	RE-1001	**Kennedy**	
Louvre	RA-153	Bobbie	CR-296
Maid	MA-564	Jackie	RA-280
Name	RA-186, RA-1002	Ted	CL-287
		Kentucky Fried Chicken	
Nazi guard,	CL-806	Liberals	RA-350
New Yorker	RA-383	Kiss	
Palm Springs	RA-390	Calcium	RU-213
Parrot	AN-386	Klu Klux Knievel	
Pay toilet	RA-692	Niggers -- XXX	RA-413
Pedophile	RA-850	Knock, knock	
Prostitute	WH-953	Fuck	CL-193
Psychiatrist	RA-322		
Rabbi's son	RE-357	**Las Vegas**	
Retiree	RA-391	Big mouth	RU-298
San Fernando Valley	CL-712	Mann Act	SE-169
Saks 5th Ave.	RA-322	Showgirl	CL-141
Spanish	RA-615	Law	
St. Patrick's Day	CL-707	Fraud	DO-568
Sunbathe	SE-999	Seagull	PG-514
Titanic	RA-542	Lawrence Welk	

Trust	RA-508	Moose	CL-672
Lawyer		Wife	MA-254,
Adulterous wife	LA-172		MA-783
Bar	BA-961	Louvre	
Birth	DO-787	Jewish	RA-153
Devil	DO-424	Luau	
Dog	AN-20	French	RU-53
God	DO-876	Lumberjack	
Horseshit -- XXX	LA-792	Lunch card	WH-38
Hostage	DO-853	Manicure	WH-399
Juror	RU-265		
Plumber	DO-308	**M&Ms**	
Pretty girl	DO-848	Falsies	CL-13
Prostitute	DO-907	Jesus	RE-651
Reduce charge	CL-229	Mailman	
Screw anybody	BA-961	Christmas	MA-402
Secretary	SE-170	Dog bite	AN-321
Time sheets	DO-516	Veteran	RU-804
United Way	CL-99	Manicure	
Lies		Cuticle	WH-399
Three Biggest	CL-435	Mann Act	
Limerick		Vegas trip	SE-169
Coitus	CL-28	Marriage	
Llama	AN-34	20 year old breasts	AN-20,
Linda Lovelace			MA-206
Hereditary	SE-381	25th anniversary	MA-96,
Masturbation	SE-372		PG-883
Lincoln		Act married	MA-826
Free slaves	RA-448	Adultery	GO-97,
Loan shark			MA-494
Massage parlor	WH-511	Affair	MA-991
Loma Linda		AIDS	DO-822
Baboon	CL-697	Aspirin	SE-626
Los Angeles		Auction	MA-276
Safest day	RA-460	Bank robbery	DO-986

Lottery		Beautiful Day	GO-977
Best man	MA-10	Memory problem	MA-836
Bonus	MA-881	Mother in law	AN-873
Boston Strangler	MA-217	Movie	MA-935
Bucking bronco fuck	RU-842	Mutual orgasm	SE-458
Cad	MA-532	Nude picture	CL-756
Cajun	SE-216	Orgasm	SE-505
Cheating	MA-29	Pearly gates	RE-164
Cock	RU-503	Say something good	MA-973
Crotchless panties	SE-703	Sexual performance	MA-212,
Difference from mistress	MA-830		MA-293, MA-314
Divorce	MA-827	Statue	MA-859
Drivig	MA-1018	Strange stuff	MA-387
Epitaph	MA-374	Victoria's Secret	SE-703
Farmer's wife	MA-484	Widow	SE-999
Fast car	MA-969	Martin Luther King	
Frigid	MA-688	Pope	RE-171
Funeral	MA-301, SE-763	School	RA-178
		Martini	
Gas station	MA-800	Drunk	RU-353, BA-893
Girdle	MA-224		
Golf	GO-338, DO-95, GO-97	Fucking	CL-134
		Masturbation	RU-664
		Testicle	CL-268
Good grammar	MA-313	Women's Breasts	CL-40
Headache	MA-397	Mary	
Heart attack	DO-252	Pregnant	RE-31
Honeymoon	MA-914	Masturbation	
Implant	MA-943	Airplane	RU-282,
Ladies night out	MA-962		RU-359
Leisure World [a retirement home]	CL-815	Beat fish	SE-467
		Castaway	RU-348
Lottery	MA-783	Competitor	RU-365
Maternity ward	CL-278	Date	RU-664

Math teacher	MA-12	Deaf Mute	SE-677
Elbow	RU-168	Quicksand	RA-813
Helen Keller	SE-454	Rowing	RE-869
Home work	SE-300	Spaniard	RA-744
Need glasses	RU-33	Texans	RA-438
Playboy	RU-282	That's Incredible	RA-758
Polish	RA-246	Twelve kids	RA-579
Rejection	RU-561	Wedding	RA-518
Self-winding watch	RU-266	Mickey Rooney	
Sperm	RU-433	Show girl	CL-141
Theatre	SE-80	Microwave	
Women	SE-522	Sodomy	SE-932
Math teachers		Midget	
Divorce	MA-12	Oral sex	WH-285
Mental Health		Military	
Support	CL-8	Drunk colonel	MI-274
Mexican		Waking up	DO-481
Barbeque	RA-621	Mistress	
Big nose	RA-598	Definition	CL-1
Cadillac	RA-360	Monkey	
Cinco De Mayo	RA-817	Space Program	AN-181
Coat & Tie	RA-687	Moose	
Cosigner	RA-813	Lawrence Welk	CL-672
Dangerous	RA-139	Rabbit	AN-182
Driver education	RA-593	Mormon	
Greaser	RA-556	Alcohol	RA-984
Hungry	RA-317	Christ returns	RE-410
Jumper cables	RA-518	Black	RA-754
Lab experiment	RA-663	Moth	
Maid	MA-564,	Ball	AN-84
	SE-1004	Light	DO-970
Marry a Polack	RA-457	Motorcycle	
Oil well fire	RA-451	Honda	RU-201
Olympics	RA-656	Neighbor's wife	CL-653
Organ grinder	RA-501	Sayings	RU-1003

Orgasm	RA-824		
Mouse		Old age	
Comparison with man	CL-138	Bingo	CL-906
In pussy	MA-447	Bladder problem	RU-260
Mushroom		Fingers	SE-137
Girl mushroom	PG-649	Incontinent wine	TO-966
		Kidney problem	CL-226
NAACP		Laundry -- XXX	MA-312
Washing Machine	RA-108	Leisure World	CL-815
Napoleon		Memory	PG-753,
Josephine	SE-487		MA-836,
NASA			CL-851
Definition of a woman	RU-498	Missing wife	MA-989
National Anthem		Nursing home	PG-685,
Singer	RU-992		RU-933
National Geographic		Once a night	PG-408
Carl Lewis	RA-702	Parkinsons	RU-933
Necrophilia		Pregnant	MA-329
Irish	SE-879	Remarriage	MA-183
New Yorker		Sixtieth birthday	RU-341
Question	PG-179	Social Security	MA-884,
Nun			SE-958
Bikini	RE-118,	Sperm bank	DO-642
	RE-161	Stairs	PG-877
Black Mother Superior	RA-595	Strawberry Sunday	MA-836
Dracula	RE-947	Strong hands	RU-503
Game Show	SE-764	Twenty-Fifth	MA-96
Sahara desert	SE-149	Anniversary	
Stewardess	RE-442	Useless thing	CL-242
Nurse		Waking up	DO-481
Head nurse	SE-519	Young wife	PG-753
Nymphomaniac		Your place or mine	PG-877
Beauty shop	SE-191	Olympics	
		Mexican	RA-656
Oil well fire		One-eyed sex fiend	RU-57

Mexican	RA-451	Oprah Winfrey	CL-773
Oral sex		Plaque	SE-552
Al Hirt	RU-294	Polish	RA-594
Asparagus	CL-679	Pope	RE-493
Belly button	SE-151	Priest	RE-975
Breathing	CL-52	Pubic hair	SE-414
Bride	SE-982	Rifle	SE-684
Broad jump	RU-64	Roses	SE-507
Cinderella	SE-115	Rug	SE-54
Cold hands	RU-919	Shy girl	SE-72
Cub scout	SE-73	Sixty eight	SE-75
Dark and lonely	SE-592	Snails	RU-371
Diaper	SE-865	Swallow	RU-818
Dog	AN-320	Taste	RU-228
Drum	SE-528	Tongue	SE-112
Ear	MA-56	Too fat	CL-680
Echo	RU-131	Tree	RU-368
First time	SE-803	UCLA	RU-297
Flees	AN-253,	View	SE-465
	RU-294	Vision	DO-327
Golf ball	SE-509	Whale	RU-868
Good grammar	MA-313	Organ grinder	
Great	SE-738	Gay	GA-215
Gynecologist	RU-840	Mexican	RA-501
Head and Shoulders	SE-486	Orgasm	
Infrequent	RU-228	Girlfriend	GO-623
Jewish	RA-453,	Mutual	SE-458
	MA-512	Sneeze	TO-210
Lies	CL-435	Wife	SE-505
Martinis	CL-268	Oriental eyes	
Mouthful	RU-286	Rice	RA-629
Napoleon	SE-487	Owl	
Nurse	SE-519	Rooster	RU-515
Orgasm	DO-152		
Orgy	RU-342	**P**acifier	

Parsley	CL-332	Rape	CL-270
Pampers		Asshole replacement	RA-249
June Allison	CL-871	Ballerina	RA-349
Pants		Bank robber	RA-401
Tight	SE-120	Birth control pills	DO-221,
Panty Hose	CL-236,		RA-355
	RU-689	Black problem	RA-233
Parachute		Blind date	RA-367
Allah	RE-417	Break finger	RA-166
Polish	RA-340	Breathalyzer	RA-482
Prostitute Club	WH-126	Burglary	RA-636
Paranoids anonymous		Burial at sea	RA-389
Meetings	PG-844	Cab ride	RA-436
Parrot		Car sex	RA-116
Adultery	AN-347	Cesarean	RA-533
Catholic	RE-980	Chicken rancher	RA-441
Israeli	AN-386	Children	RA-923
Parsley		Choir	RA-571
Pussy	CL-332	Coal miner	RA-328
Peanuts		Counting	RA-256
Son-in-law	MA-231	Deodorant	RA-380
Peanut Butter		Diarrhea	RA-504
Donkey	AN-237	Driving	RA-351,
Pussy	RA-779		RA-385
Pedophile		Drug addicts	RA-766
Girlfriend	TO-945	Drunk driving	RA-482
Pepper		Evil Kowalski	RA-394
Use	TO-210	Eye chart	RA-375
Pick up lines	RU-946	Farmer's daughter	RA-411
Pigeons		FBI	RA-431
Flying upside down	CL-444	Fish	RA-362
Wife	MA-859	Foreplay	RA-614
Polar bear		Gatorade	RA-395
Baby	AN-928	Get pregnant	RA-356
Polish		Godfather	RA-346,

Abortion Clinic	RA-412		RA-378
Gorilla	RA-392	Panties	RA-536
Graduation	RA-870	Parachute	RA-340
Gross ignorance	RA-537	Peeping Tom	RA-354
Guerrilla	RA-478, RA-550	Penis shape	RA-382
		Penis transplant	RA-423
Hand grenade	RA-478	Poland, discoverer	RA-255
Hearing AIDS	RA-762	Police line up	RA-403
Honeymoon	RA-328	Pope	RA-489
Horseshit	RA-440	Post office jobs -- XXX	RA-344
Hunting	RA-273	Potato	RA-574
Hurricane	RA-825	Proctologist	RA-694
Impregnate	RA-590	Rape	RA-477
Intelligence test	RA-176, DO-263	Revolutionary	RA-550
		Right Guard	RA-380
Javelin team	RA-525	Sausage	RA-323, RA-538
Jesus	RA-543, RA-736	Screw on backs	RA-695
Joke	RA-489	Seamen/urine	RA-364
Kotex	RA-616	Sex manual	RA-420
Language	RA-597	Sleeping bag	RA-531
Lesbian	RA-772	Sleeping in barn	AN-361
Lies	RA-709	Social climber	RA-194
Light bulb	RA-195	Spiritualist	RA-606
Lottery	RA-765	Sucking thumb	RA-214
Marriage proposal	RA-535	Telephone poles	RA-925
Married	RA-396	Turtle neck sweater	RA-281
Marry Mexican	RA-457	Vibrator	RA-476
Masturbation	RA-246	Walking a breast	RA-422
Menstruating	RA-310	War bride	RA-334
Mine detector	RA-333	Watermelon	RA-854
Mother-in-law	RA-530	Wedding	RA-232
Mother's Day	RU-407	Wedding announcement	RA-562
Oral sex	RA-594		
Outhouse	RA-376	Whorehouse	RA-209

Pacemaker	RA-450		
Politics		Cops	SE-849
Biden	PO-771	Definition	SE-466
Carter, Jackson	RA-491	Drip dry	SE-78
Clinton	RE-638,	Elephant trunk	RU-862
	SE-746,	Irish arthritis	RA-58
	PO-782,	Jewish	RA-44
	PG-897,	Madam whorehouse	WH-94
	PO-905,	Medium/Rare	CL-708
	PO-908,	Owl	RU-515
	PO-917,	Potato	CL-591
	RA-922	Small	RU-202,
Dolly Parton	CL-668		RU-223
Fonda	PG-897	Stick up	PG-79,
Hillary	PO-899,		CL-553
	PO-918	Shorts	RU-582
Jessie Jackson	RA-798	Vaseline	DO-136
John Edwards	PO-905	Wrinkles	CL-705
Pres. Ford	PO-418	Young/old	RU-503
Roe v. Wade	PO-821	Priest	
Sen. Benson	PO-797	Baseball	MA-952
Pope		Bikini	RE-161
Blowjob	RE-493	Camel	SE-149
Christ returns	RE-410	Confessional	RE-975
Driving a car	PO-886	Golf	DO-150
Heaven	RE-607	Hospital	DO-175
Polish	RA-489	Last Rites	DO-175
Virgin Mary	RE-638	Nun/Camel	SE-149
Preacher		Parrots	RE-980
Hearing	RE-995	Pimple	RE-957
Hypnotist	RE-133	Swimming lesson	RE-927
Prick		Prince Charles Wedding	
All of it	SE-225	Queen	GA-967
Big	WH-285	Prostitute	
Black	RA-700	Cab	WH-83

Cobra	CL-674	Computer	CL-100
Elephant	WH-102	Son	RE-15,
Eye out	WH-147		RE-357
Las Vegas	RU-298	Rape	
Loan shark	WH-511	Black -- XXX	DO-11
Make hot	WH-330	Ratchet	
Molested	WH-895	Definition	CL-130
Old/young	CL-305	Red Cross	
Parachute club	WH-126	Flood	PG-132
Pitbull	SE-786	Red neck	
Runny nose	WH-898	Baptism	RE-23
Sailor	WH-882	Chains	RA-22
Weatherman special	WH-17	Genie	RA-934
Pussy		Trash truck	RA-416
Auction	MA-276	Religion	
Cunt	RU-889	Baptist	RE-959
Fat woman	SE-474	Bears	AN-784
Itchy	RU-735	Cast first stone	RE-198
Jewish	RA-44	Christian Pilot	RE-417
Mouse	MA-447	Commandments	CL-358
Nigger -- XXX	RA-661	Doctor	DO-445
Polish	RA-376	Eve	RU-569
Pussy	RE-430	Gays, debate	GA-676
Pubic hair	SE-414	God return	RE-219
Smell	MA-935,	Jesus name	RA-234
	RU-994	Mexicans	RE-869
Stretcher	RU-70	Monastery cat	RE-608
Superiority	CL-304	Mountain climber	RE-419
UCLA	RU-297	pastor	
		Oral sex	SE-552
Rabbi		Pope	RE-493
Christ returns	RE-160	Report card	
Convert black	RE-159	Child	RA-283
Golf	RE-425,	Restaurant	
	RA-874	Chinese	RA-177

Hawaiian vacation	RE-972	Soup	RU-154
Restroom		Scholarship	
Incontinent man	RU-260	Black	RA-180
Robot		Science	
Female	RU-809	Bras	RU-964
Rock Hudson		School	
Baseball	GA-740	Homework	SE-300
Cremation	GA-720	Report card	RA-283
Getting better	GA-721	Texas girls	CL-197
Insurance	GA-718	Scottish soldier	
Statue of liberty	GA-745	Gay	MI-146
Wallet	GA-729	Scotch	
Rolls Royce		Tits	CL-324
BMW	PO-887	Scouts	
Rooster		Cub scout	SE-73
Owl	RU-515	Secretary	
Telephone pole	CL-710	Executive	CL-4,
Roses			RU-805
Blond	CL-963	Good news/bad news	SE-377
Roto rooter		Senior sex	
Poland	RA-255	Honeymoon	MA-183
		Pregnant	MA-329
Sammy Davis Jr.		Remarriage	SE-137
Bo Derek	RA-603	Strong hands	RU-503
Eye patch	RA-46	Urinal	RU-341
Hemmoroidectomy	RA-211	Useless	CL-242
Sailor		Wash clothes -- XXX	MA-312
knots	CL-3,	25th Anniversary	MA-96,
	WH-882		PG-883
Pig, difference	RU-632	Sex	
Salem		Asparagus	CL-679
Country	CL-318	Blind date	SE-978
Sanitary belt		Conception	DO-335
Definition	CL-162	Desert Island	RU-336
Schizophrenic		Doctor, frequency	DO-339

Definition -- XXX	CL-45	Dog style	AN-262,
Dog style cont.	MA-682	Motto	RU-368
Ear	MA-56	Skunk, blind	
Epitaphs	MA-374	Fart	SE-734
Feel like a woman	RU-911	Skyjacking	
Female doctor	DO-343	Crime	RU-359
Fiend	RU-57	Sleeping bag	
First sex act	CL-307	Polack	RA-531
French luau	RU-53	Slut	
Frequency	PG-36	Definition	RU-793
Golf ball	SE-509	Smoking	
Medicare	DO-316	Breast cancer	TO-74
Misdemeanor	RU-369	girls who smoke	RU-291
Nurse	SE-519	Salem	CL-318
Oral, tulips	SE-507	Snail Tail	
Orgasm	DO-152	Woman	RU-497
Pill	MA-212	Snowman	
Plaque	SE-552	Snowwoman	PG-544
Relations	MA-240	Snowstorm	
Smoking	RU-291	Like sex	SE-547
Son-in-law	MA-231	Snow White	
Swinging singles	SE-326	St. Peter	DO-158
Ugly woman	SE-379	Social climber	
Vaseline	MA-55	Polack	RA-194
VW	DO-335	Social Security Sex	SE-958
Zip code	RU-366	Sodomy	
Shakespeare	CL-207	Charge reduced	CL-229
Shoes		Son in law	
Italians	RA-863	Should be	MA-231
Short people		Space program	
Showgirl	CL-141	Blacks	AN-181
Siamese Twin		Spaghetti	
England	PG-860	Chef Boyardee	
Sickle cell anemia		Speech Code	
Cause	TO-415	Sperm	

255

Sierra Club		Race	
Sperm bank		French	CL-358
Senior	DO-642	Texan	CL-268
Spider		Alligator -- XXX	AN-51
Queer	AN-35	Arab	RU-370
St. Peter		Camel	AN-6
Man of the house	RE-164	Girl's finishing schools	CL-197
Star Trek		Gorilla	RA-624
Toilet paper	RU-617	Mexicans	RA-438
Streaker		Okies	RA-438
Strutter	CL-388	Thanksgiving	PG-864
Superman		That's Incredible	
Meets drunk	SE-609	Mexicans	RA-758
Swearing		Thermometer	
Complaints	BA-554	Doctor	DO-87
		Throat	
Tampax	CL-521	Linda Lovelace	SE-372
Elephant	AN-572	Tiger	
Genie	RA-303	Definition	SE-452
Kotex	RA-616	Titanic	
String	RU-774	Jews	RA-542
Tea Bag	RU-770	Linda Lovelace	SE-381
Tarzan		Mexico/Polack	SE-372
Jane	RU-750	Toilet paper	
Italian/polish	RA-678	Implants	MA-943
Tattoo		Star Trek	RU-617
Woman's thighs	BA-517	Toilet seat	RU-617
TB		Flea	CL-16
How tell	RU-409	Woman	CL-16
Teacher		Tongue	
Al Sharpton	RA-178	Sex organ	RU-658
Telephone		Topless bathing suit	
Mexican maid	MA-564	Wash it	SE-112
Polack/Italian	RA-925	Tranquilizer	

Rooster	CL-710	Aphrodisiac	CL-125
Ten Commandants			
Transplant		Farmer	AN-648
Polack	CL-124	Veterinarian	
Traveling salesmen		Patient	DO-1000
Loyalty test	RA-249	Viagra	
Tuba		Druggist	DO-956
Drunk	PG-39	Generic name	RU-968
Tulips		Vibrator	
Roses	RU-241	Elephant	AN-640
		Polish	RA-476

UCLA

		Scottish	RA-954
Eating pussy	RU-297	Vietnam	
Honor system	CR-920	Clinton	PG-897
Uncle		Cookbook	RA-529
Four balls	RU-59	Virgin	
Union boss		Hemophiliac	CL-675
Whorehouse	WH-292	Waterbed	CL-693
Union Carbide		Virgin birth	
Company song	RA-699	God visit earth	RE-219
Urinal		Virgin Mary	
Rabbi	RE-155	Bill Clinton	RE-638
		VW	

Vagina

		Conception	DO-335
See "Pussy"		Tiger in	CL-99
Valley Girl			
Ears	CL-669		

Waitress

Vampire		Anheuser Busch	RU-752
Tea bag	RU-770	BLT	RU-405
Vaseline		Menu	RU-633
Erection	DO-136	Waterbed	
Polygrip	CL-305	Virgin	CL-693
Use	MA-55	JAP	RA-634
VD		Watermelon	
Or TB	RU-409	Black	RA-613

Ventriloquist		Chinese	RA-769
Blonde	CL-976	Polish	RA-854
Waterskiing		Italian	MA-24
Black	RA-114	Movie rental	MA-935
Weatherman		Painful intercourse	MA-47
Prostitute	WH-17	Pearly Gates	RE-164
Wedding		Queer	MA-56
Best man	MA-10	Willie Nelson	
Weight loss clinic		Tattoo	BA-517
Attendant	RA-148	Wine	
Welfare check		Incontinent	TO-966
Endorse -- XXX	RA-189	Witch	
Welk, Lawrence		Golden Gate Bridge	CL-61
Moose	CL-672	Bite ear	CL-135
Whale		Women	
Circumcise	AN-627	Battered	TO-833
Whiplash		Bitch	RU-749
Israeli war	RA-230	Computer	RU-942
Whistle		Dumb	RU-660
Bar	TO-428	Feel like	RU-911
Whores See "Prostitute"		Life support	RU-498
Whorehouse		Masturbation	SE-522
Big prick	WH-94, WH-285	Perfect	RU-596
		Pick up	RU-971
Chicken	AN-144	PMS	AN-838
Drunk	WH-95	Toilet seat	RU-658
Glass eye	WH-147	Two sets of lips	CL-904
Polish	RA-209	Unique	RU-921
Quadriplegic	WH-267	Wooden Eye	
Small prick	WH-19	Wedding proposal	RU-250
Union	WH-292	Woody Allen	
Wife		Movie	CL-900
Bathroom scale	MA-969		
Battered	TO-833		
Country club	CL-713		

Frigid MA-688
Gas station attendant MA-800

Yogurt
California PG-875

Zipper
Med Fly DO-620

Browse all the jokes online, including the XXX jokes, leave comments, and store your own jokes and favorites with an online subscription to www.dadsjokebook.com. Register your book purchase and receive 20% off your annual membership.

Made in the USA
Monee, IL
20 November 2020